Recent Themes in American Religious History

Historians in Conversation:
Recent Themes in Understanding the Past
Series editor, Louis A. Ferleger

Recent Themes in

AMERICAN RELIGIOUS HISTORY

Historians in Conversation

Edited by Randall J. Stephens

The University of South Carolina Press

Published by the University of South Carolina Press
Columbia, South Carolina 29208

www.sc.edu/uscpress

Manufactured in the United States of America

18 17 16 15 14 13 12 11 10 09 10 9 8 7 6 5 4 3 2 1

Library of Congress Cataloging-in-Publication Data

Recent themes in American religious history : historians in conversation /
edited by Randall J. Stephens.
p. cm. — (Historians in conversation)
Includes bibliographical references (p.) and index.
ISBN 978-1-57003-869-3 (pbk : alk. paper)
1. United States—Religion. I. Stephens, Randall J., 1973–
BL2525.R42 1977
277.3'08—dc22
2009026126

This book was printed on Glatfelter Natures, a recycled paper with 30 percent postconsumer waste content.

Contents

Series Editor's Preface

The Historical Society was founded in 1997 to create more venues for common conversations about the past. Consequently, in the autumn of 2001, the Historical Society launched a new type of publication. The society's president, George Huppert, and I believed that there was an important niche for a publication that would make the work of the most prominent historians more accessible to nonspecialists and general readers. We recruited two historians who shared this vision, Joseph S. Lucas and Donald A. Yerxa, and asked them to transform *Historically Speaking* into a journal of historical ideas. Up to that point *Historically Speaking* had served as an in-house publication reporting on the society's activities and its members' professional accomplishments. Yerxa and Lucas quickly changed the layout and content of *Historically Speaking,* and within a short period of time many of the most prominent historians in the world began appearing in its pages—people such as Danielle Allen, Niall Ferguson, Daniel Walker Howe, Mary Lefkowitz, Pauline Maier, William McNeill, Geoffrey Parker, and Sanjay Subrahmanyam. *Historically Speaking*'s essays, forums, and interviews have drawn widespread attention. The *Chronicle of Higher Education*'s Magazine and Journal Reader section, for example, repeatedly has highlighted pieces appearing in *Historically Speaking.* And leading historians are loyal readers, praising *Historically Speaking* as a "must-read" journal, a "*New York Review of Books* for history," and "the most intellectually exciting publication in history that is currently available."

The Historical Society is pleased to partner with the University of South Carolina Press to publish a multivolume series *Historians in Conversation: Recent Themes in Understanding the Past.* Each thematic volume pulls key essays, forums, and interviews from *Historically Speaking* and makes them accessible for classroom use and for the general reader. The original selections from *Historically Speaking* are supplemented with an introductory essay by Randall J. Stephens along with suggestions for further reading.

We welcome your interest in the Historical Society. You may find us on the Internet at bu.edu/historic. You may also contact us at the Historical Society, 656 Beacon St., Mezzanine, Boston, Mass., 02215-2010, telephone 617-358-0260.

LOUIS A. FERLEGER

Acknowledgments

Since I first started as an associate editor of *Historically Speaking* in 2005, I've had the pleasure of working with a number of historians of American religion. Their many insights have prodded me on, both as a teacher and a scholar. This project could not have seen the light of day without the encouragement and wisdom of many, including Randall Balmer, Chris Beneke, Maura Jane Farrelly, Lou Ferleger, Philip Goff, Scott Hovey, Joe Lucas, Charles Marsh, Robert Orsi, Stephen Prothero, Jon Roberts, Beth Stephens, John Turner, Grant Wacker, Brian Ward, Bland Whitely, Anne Wyatt-Brown, Bert Wyatt-Brown, and Donald Yerxa.

From 2007 to 2009 I was lucky enough to be part of the Young Scholars in American Religion Program at the Center for the Study of Religion and American Culture, Indiana University–Purdue University of Indianapolis. Every semester nine other early-career scholars and I would meet up to discuss teaching, share our research, play a little touch football in the shadow of the towering Lucas Oil Stadium, and talk into the wee hours of the night about our lives outside the walls of the academy. Our very generous mentors, Paul Harvey and Amanda Porterfield, could not have been better suited to lead us. I thank Paul and Amanda and my fellow YSARers—Edward J. Blum, Darren Dochuk, Katherine Carté Engel, J. Spencer Fluhman, Rebecca Goetz, Charles F. Irons, Kathryn Lofton, Matthew A. Sutton, and Tisa J. Wenger—for their advice, knowledge shared on this book and other projects, and friendship.

Introduction

American Religious History in Context

Randall J. Stephens

Along with Jimmy Carter, George W. Bush ranks as one of the most openly Christian, even evangelical, presidents in American history. Bush was frank about his faith in his 1999 campaign autobiography, *A Charge to Keep*. In it the future president described revivals he attended and the Episcopal and Presbyterian churches where he worshipped as a youth. Bush noted his switch to the Methodist church, where he and Laura tied the knot. America's premier revivalist, Billy Graham, shaped Bush's spiritual life more than any other person. The evangelist visited with Bush's family in Maine in 1985. "He led me to the path," Bush recalled years later. "And it was the beginning of a change in my life. I had always been a religious person, had regularly attended church, even taught Sunday school and served as an altar boy." But under Graham's religious tutelage, he recommitted his heart to Jesus.

There was another, unofficial story of Bush's conversion. The second version did not include one of the most recognizable Christians in the country. A year before he met with Graham, Bush requested a meeting with Arthur Blessitt, an eccentric, itinerant evangelical who had become famous for carrying a twelve-foot cross around the world. According to this account, confirmed by Karl Rove, Bush's chief advisor, Blessitt and Bush met at the empty Holidome restaurant of a west Texas Holiday Inn. Blessitt recalls asking the younger Bush: "If you died this moment, do you have the assurance you would go to heaven?" "No," Bush responded. "Then let me explain to you how you can have that assurance and know for sure that you are saved," Blessitt pleaded. The meeting reportedly ended with the two men holding hands and Blessitt praying for Bush's salvation.[1]

Regardless of which conversion story mattered most to Bush and his handlers, the future president spoke the language of evangelicalism, a movement that claims roughly one-third of all Americans. It was also a movement that had grown dramatically and gained a great deal of prestige from the colonial era when Baptists and Methodists remained, to a great extent, cultural and religious outsiders. The success of evangelicalism reveals the dynamic role religion continues to play in America and shines light on the shifting place of religion in American public life.

Methodism, the quintessential evangelical religion, became the premier denomination in America in the early nineteenth century and would later help produce Pentecostalism, an even-larger religious movement that now has half a billion followers worldwide. The religion of the heart has grown tremendously in America since the 1970s, an era some wags labeled the "born-again" decade. Evangelicals preach a personalist faith. Believers claim that they know God intimately. The creator of the universe might guide stalwarts' every move from choice of spouse to political affiliation. In 2000, 68 percent of evangelicals voted for George W. Bush; in 2004, 78 percent did so.[2]

One wonders what the late social historian E. P. Thompson, the son of Methodist missionaries, might think of this recent surge. Thompson would probably find little to praise in America's largely conservative, mass religious movement. Indeed he famously dismissed early Methodism in his classic *The Making of the English Working Class* as little more than "a ritualized form of psychic masturbation."[3]

This was not the opinion of Thompson alone. Indeed the leading scholars of the nineteenth century—including Auguste Comte, Herbert Spencer, Emile Durkheim, Max Weber, Karl Marx, and Sigmund Freud—believed that religion would eventually wane with the steady march of progress. Through most of the twentieth century, the secularization thesis—a view that Westerners were becoming less and less religious with the advance of science and the decline of superstition and institutional religion—dominated the social sciences and served as a master model. C. Wright Mills ably summed up the views of many when in 1959 he wrote, "Once the world was filled with the sacred—in thought, practice, and institutional form. After the Reformation and the Renaissance, the forces of modernization swept across the globe and secularization, a corollary historical process, loosened the dominance of the sacred. In due course, the sacred shall disappear altogether except, possibly, in the private realm."[4]

Much has changed since Mills wrote the above prophecy and since Thompson penned his legendary rebuke against holy-rolling onanism. The secularization thesis has come under attack for its inability to explain the power and reach of religion in the modern era. Retractions were in order.

"The assumption that we live in a secularized world is false," wrote sociologist Peter L. Berger, once a fierce champion of secularization theory. "The world today, with some exceptions . . . is as furiously religious as it ever was, and in some places more so than ever." At the same time ever-greater numbers of historians and sociologists are studying the role of religion in America, past and present. Stanley Fish sensed the growing importance of religion in the wake of the September 11, 2001, terrorist attacks: "When Jacques Derrida died I was called by a reporter who wanted to know what would succeed high theory and the triumvirate of race, gender, and class as the center of intellectual energy in the academy. I answered like a shot: religion."[5]

Even the most materialist of scholars today seems willing to pay attention to the vital, real role religion plays in the lives of millions around the globe. The study of American religion has gained in credibility in the last three decades. Indeed some of the most provocative work in American history today is in the subfield of religious history. Much has been written of late on groups that once received little attention. Histories of Mormonism, Catholicism, Native American spirituality, and Judaism continue to multiply as well as studies on the religious lives of women, African Americans, Hispanics, and other minorities. The study of religion and sexuality is now also a rewarding area of research.[6]

One of the most promising new developments is the work on what some call "lived religion." Since the 1980s and 1990s, religious historians have increasingly turned their attention to how American men and women, young and old, practice their faith on a day-to-day basis. Formal theology and institution building are less important in such accounts. The works of David D. Hall on folk religion and magic in colonial America, Paul Harvey and Charles Marsh on black religion and southern culture, and Nancy Ammerman on American Baptists in the twentieth century are fitting examples of this recent approach. Religious studies scholar and historian Colleen McDannell has summarized this development. Since the 1980s historians of religion have turned their attention to religious practice, ranging "from formal, communal rituals with long histories to spontaneous actions that an individual may understand as religious." McDannell notes, "Religious practices are visceral and sensual. They involve the body in action."[7]

McDannell also stresses the importance of the wide range of religious actors now being studied. American religious history written from the "bottom up" is a relatively recent, yet growing, phenomenon. Newly minted Ph.D.s make up the larger portion of American religion scholars. Some analyze the religious lives of the poor and dispossessed in the nineteenth century, others examine the material religion of colonial America or the religious roots of the modern civil rights movement. In 2007 four leading scholars considered "How the Graduate Study of Religion and American Culture Has Changed in the Past Decade." Participants in this forum, which appeared in the journal *Religion and American Culture,* answered a variety of questions as they assessed the shape of things: "What has changed in the graduate curriculum in the past decade? How have faculty appointments reflected changing patterns? Have student interests shifted over this time period?" On the West Coast Catherine L. Albanese noted that students increasingly wanted to study "religion on the ground." These students had less and less interest in traditional church-history topics and the standard seminary curriculum of ages past. Graduate students gravitated to interdisciplinary topics and looked for global and transatlantic components of American religion. Leigh Eric Schmidt saw a similar development at Princeton: "The study of American religious history is more than a wing of American studies or area studies; it involves the history of ideas, institutions, and cultures that transcend the geographic borders and temporal parameters of 'America' or the 'Americas.'" At Duke University and the University of North Carolina, Chapel Hill, Thomas Tweed also observed a broadening of the field. Graduate students at those institutions focused on white Protestant diversity as well as Mormonism, Catholicism, and the Nation of Islam. Their work revealed how the study of religion in the United States was becoming a multidisciplinary field in the humanities and social sciences.[8]

How have these developments shaped the field of American history? The American Historical Association tracks areas of study for twenty-five thousand historians at universities and historical agencies in Canada and the United States. Members may designate three topical fields of interest. James M. O'Toole's research on this subject, included in the current volume, reveals that in 2006, 918 historians listed work on religion. That number was second only to those who categorized themselves as cultural historians.[9]

American religious history books also win prizes, an indication of religious history's place in the larger field. Since 1983 five American religious history titles have won the Bancroft Prize, besides the Pulitzer, the most prestigious award for historians. Awards such as the Templeton Prize—at $1.6 million it is the largest annual award given for intellectual merit—and the Grawenmeyer Award—that includes a $200,000 prize—are within reach of those who work on religion in America. Additional funds for researchers come from the John Templeton Foundation and the Lilly Endowment among others. Maybe more important, for cash-strapped scholars, as an editor at Harvard University Press recently remarked, religious history sells. Yet are the larger fields of American history and American studies buying?

Maybe not—some historians think that the story of American religion is not yet a significant part of the larger narrative of American history. In their view American historians and American studies scholars still have not integrated religion into the story of modern America. Religious topics fit comfortably into pre-1870 American history: the Puritans, Salem witch trials, great awakenings, denominational expansion, and social reform. As Jon Butler notes, after 1870 "religion more often appears as a jack-in-the-box, whether in U.S. history textbooks or survey course lectures." Religion pops up here and there and then retreats back into the box. Topics and individuals like the Scopes Trial, Martin Luther King Jr., and the rise of the New Right get some attention but little deep reflection. Butler astutely observes, "Textbooks rarely connect American religious figures and events between 1870 and 2000 to larger enduring patterns in American life."[10]

A look at the larger world of scholarship shows something similar. Key academic publications like the *American Quarterly* and the *Journal of American History* rarely include American religious history topics. In a recent ten-year span only 5 percent of the articles in the *American Quarterly,* the premier publication for American studies, covered religious history. Only 4.3 percent of the essays in the *Journal of American History* dealt with religion over the same period.[11]

John T. McGreevy argues that because historians long studied the post–Civil War era through the lenses of politics (the triumph of a liberal, activist government) and organizational developments (the bureaucratization of American life), religion remained epiphenomenal.[12] George Marsden, Notre Dame historian and author of a Bancroft Prize–winning biography of colonial America theologian Jonathan Edwards, sees something similar at play. The story of American religion has run counter to the inevitable secularization scholars long predicted, says Marsden. In his view, though, "exclusivists forms of Christianity and other faiths seem to become *more popular* as the nation modernizes." The rapid growth of free churches, megachurches, and Pentecostalism, Marsden argues, does not square with a master narrative of diversity and tolerance.[13]

This neglect actually has much to do with the kinds of religious groups and theologies that capture the imaginations of historians. Hence religious studies scholars have tended to focus on articulate religious bodies and groups that were pertinent to their own academic interests. Historian of American religion Robert Orsi maintains that religious studies departments have all too often been "departments of the study of desirable religion."[14]

Why? Perhaps academics' unfamiliarity with or disdain for ecstatic and/or conservative religion accounts for the oversight. Take, for example, the American Christian bookstore, a place that few academics would ever venture into or even be aware of. There are thousands of Christian bookstores scattered across the country. They showcase the power and popularity of an increasingly self-contained, parallel culture. These bookstores are virtually nonexistent in leading cultural centers like New York, Chicago, Los Angeles, San Francisco, and Boston. Yet the Family Christian Stores chain, to take but one example, has over five thousand employees and 320 locations in thirty-nine states. At its branches, and thousands of similar stores, Christian consumers purchase the standard fare: Bibles, religious art, and calendars. They also buy Christian T-shirts (some called "witness gear" with passages of scripture scrawled across them), Christian music (including easy listening, speed metal, goth, indie, and every genre in between), self-help books, and any other bauble or memento that has the name of Jesus on it. These mementoes have been termed "Jesus Junk" by one scholar. Such outlets stocked millions of copies of Hal Lindsey's apocalyptic thriller *The Late Great Planet Earth* (1970), the nonfiction bestseller of the "me decade." The publisher reports selling twenty-eight million copies of the book, though it appeared only later on the *New York Times* best-seller list. And so, the world that millions of Americans inhabit remains terra incognita to historians at American colleges and universities.[15]

There are still other reasons to take note of religion's powerful role in American society. In addition to the advance of evangelical Christianity, the landscape of traditional American religion has changed dramatically since the 1960s.[16] Such changes, though, are far more familiar to many academics than the uncharted waters of evangelicalism. "It began with the 'new immigration,' spurred by the Immigration and Nationality Act of 1965," writes religion scholar Diana L. Eck. The limits imposed by the exclusionary Immigration Act of 1924 were now a thing of the past. Cities like Dearborn, Michigan—with its concentration of Muslim immigrants—and Flushing Queens, New York—one of the most religiously diverse cities in the United States—exemplified a new pluralism. A reporter for the *New York Times* remarked, "If America really is a melting pot, Flushing seems one place where it's on a high boil. . . . Today Flushing is chock-a-block with many Protestant and Roman Catholic churches, a few synagogues, several Hindu temples, a beautiful mosque and a brand new Buddhist temple." Eck observes that now one can find Hindu, Buddhist, Jain, Sikh, Zoroastrian, African, and Afro-Caribbean centers of worship across the country. "The people of these living traditions of faith have moved into American neighborhoods, tentatively at first, their altars and prayer rooms in storefronts and office buildings, basements and garages, recreation rooms and coat closets, nearly invisible to the rest of us." Since 1991 Eck has headed the Pluralism Project at Harvard University, which explores the changing contours of American religion.[17]

Questions still persist about just how religiously plural America actually is. According to a 2007 survey conducted by the Pew Forum on Religion and Public Life, religious movements that are relatively new to the American scene represent only a fraction of the country's faith traditions. Buddhists constitute .7 percent of those surveyed while Hindus total a mere .4 percent. Muslims account for only .6 percent of America's believers. However, there is much exciting work being done on non-Western religions. Some historians like Stephen Prothero and Richard Hughes Seager trace the complex roots of Buddhism in America. Other scholars like Thomas Tweed, Robert Orsi, and Karen McCarthy Brown expertly use ethnography to reveal intricate realignments and religious fusions taking place in America's thriving cities.[18]

Scholars who write about America's traditional, conservative religious bodies are doing some of the most interesting work today. Hence the current volume contains a number of essays on evangelicalism, one of the strongest traditions in modern America, and Catholicism, a branch of Christianity that claims nearly 24 percent of Americans. Other pieces here deal with Judaism, millennialism, the limits of history, and new currents in American religious history. The essays and interviews do not provide a comprehensive picture of religion in America, a task well beyond the parameters here. This volume includes little material on non-Western religions and Native American spirituality, though the list of further readings does provide some sources on other traditions and movements. The following selections offer much insight on new directions in American religious history. Several essays examine groups and individuals that have received scant attention to date. Each author and interviewee herein is, in one way or another, addressing some of the concerns that Jon Butler has raised, placing religious history at the center of the American history narrative.[19]

Notes

1. George W. Bush and Mickey Herskowitz, *A Charge to Keep: My Journey to the White House* (New York: Harper Paperbacks, 2001), 1; Alan Cooperman, "Openly Religious, to a Point: Bush Leaves the Specifics of His Faith to Speculation," *Washington Post,* September 16, 2004, http://www.washingtonpost.com/ac2/wp-dyn/A24634–2004Sep15?language=printer (accessed December 15, 2008).

2. Frances FitzGerald, "The Evangelical Surprise," *New York Review of Books,* April 26, 2007, 31.

3. E. P. Thompson, *The Making of the English Working Class* (New York: Penguin Books, 1980), 405.

4. C. Wright Mills, *The Sociological Imagination* (New York: Oxford University Press, 1959), 32–33. See also essays in William H. Swatos and Daniel V. A. Olson, eds., *The Secularization Debate* (Lanham, Md.: Rowman & Littlefield, 2000); David Martin, *On Secularization: Towards a Revised General Theory* (Aldershot, U.K.: Ashgate Publishing, 2005); Charles Taylor, *A Secular Age* (Cambridge, Mass.: Harvard University Press, 2007); C. John Sommerville, "Secular Society Religious Population: Our Tacit Rules for Using the Term Secularization," *Journal for the Scientific Study of Religion* 37, no. 2 (1998): 249–53; and Peter L. Berger, ed., *The Desecularization of the World: Resurgent Religion and World Politics* (Grand Rapids, Mich.: Eerdmans, 1999).

5. Peter L. Berger, *The Desecularization of the World: Resurgent Religion and World Politics* (Grand Rapids, Mich.: Eerdmans, 1999), 2. Stanley Fish, "One University, under God?" *Chronicle of Higher Education,* January 7, 2005, http://chronicle.com/weekly/v51/i18/18c00101.htm (accessed May 6, 2008).

6. For overviews of recent scholarship in religious history, see Robert A. Orsi, George Marsden, David W. Wills, Colleen McDannell, "Forum: The Decade Ahead in Scholarship," *Religion and American Culture* 3, no. 1 (1993): 1–28; Martin E. Marty, "American Religious History in the Eighties: A Decade of Achievement," *Church History* 63, no. 3 (1993): 340–46 for Catholicism; 346–48 for Judaism; 348–50 for Latter-day Saints; and 350–53 for minorities; Leigh E. Schmidt, Deborah Dash Moore, Richard T. Hughes, and Mark Valeri, "The Years Ahead in Scholarship," *Religion and American Culture* 13, no. 1 (2003): 1–25; and Catherine L. Albanese, "American Religious History: A Bibliographical Essay," in *Currents in American Scholarship* (Washington, D.C.: Department of State, 2002).

7. David D. Hall, ed., *Lived Religion in America: Toward a History of Practice* (Princeton, N.J.: Princeton University Press, 1997); David D. Hall, *Worlds of Wonder, Days of Judgment: Popular Religious Belief in Early New England* (Cambridge, Mass.: Harvard University Press, 1990); Paul Harvey, *Freedom's Coming: Religious Culture and the Shaping of the South from the Civil War through the Civil Rights Era* (Chapel Hill: University of North Carolina Press, 2005); Charles Marsh, *God's Long Summer: Stories of Faith and Civil Rights* (Princeton, N.J.: Princeton University Press, 1997); Nancy Ammerman, *Bible Believers: Fundamentalists in the Modern World* (New Brunswick, N.J.: Rutgers University Press, 1987). Colleen McDannell, introduction, in *Religions of the United States in Practice,* vol. 1, ed. McDannell (Princeton, N.J.: Princeton University Press, 2001), 2.

8. Catherine L. Albanese, W. Clark Gilpin, Leigh E. Schmidt, and Thomas A. Tweed, "Forum: How the Graduate Study of Religion and American Culture Has Changed in the Past Decade," *Religion and American Culture: A Journal of Interpretation* 17, no. 1 (2007): 1, 17, 20, 25.

9. James M. O'Toole, "Religious History in the Post-Ahlstrom Era," *Historically Speaking: The Bulletin of the Historical Society* 8 (January/February 2007): 16.

10. Jon Butler, "Jack-in-the-Box Faith: The Religion Problem in Modern American History," *Journal of American History* 90, no. 4 (2004), www.historycooperative.org/journals/jah/90.4/butler.html. Simon Schama's sprawling exploration of American exceptionalism devotes pages to Roger Williams and toleration in colonial America, though Billy Graham—perhaps the most recognizable figure in modern American religion—receives only a passing notice. Simon Schama, *The American Future: A History* (New York: Ecco, 2009).

11. These figures were compiled after a March 2007 survey by the author of issues of the *American Quarterly* and the *Journal of American History* from 1997–2007. See also the third edition of Mary Beth Norton and Pamela Gerardi, eds., *The American Historical Association's Guide to Historical Literature* (New York: Oxford University Press, 1995). Religious history topics catalogued in the *Guide* are far more prevalent from the colonial era to the nineteenth century than in later periods.

12. John T. McGreevy, "Faith and Morals in the United States, 1865–Present," *Reviews in American History* 26, no. 1 (1998): 241, 242.

13. George Marsden, "Can Jonathan Edwards (and His Heirs) Be Integrated into the American History Narrative?" *Historically Speaking: The Bulletin of the Historical Society* 5 (July/August 2004): 13.

14. Robert A. Orsi, *Between Heaven and Earth: The Religious Worlds People Make and the Scholars Who Study Them* (Princeton, N.J.: Princeton University Press, 2005), 190. See also Randall J. Stephens, "Beyond the Niebuhrs: An Interview with Robert Orsi on Recent Trends in American Religious History," *Historically Speaking: The Bulletin of the Historical Society* 7 (July/August 2006): 8–11. This interview is included in part 1 of the current volume.

15. Paul Boyer, *When Time Shall Be No More: Prophecy Belief in American Culture* (Cambridge, Mass.: Harvard University Press, 1992), 5.

16. Patrick Allitt, *Religion in America since 1945: A History* (New York: Columbia University Press, 2005), 116–47.

17. Diana L. Eck, *A New Religious America: How a "Christian Country" Has Become the World's Most Religiously Diverse Nation* (New York: HarperOne, 2001), 1; John Strausbaugh, "The Melting Pot on a High Boil in Flushing," May 2, 2008, http://www.nytimes.com/2008/05/02/arts/02expl.html?_r=1&pagewanted=1 (accessed December 1, 2008).

18. For critiques of Eck's pluralist argument, see Richard John Neuhaus, "One Nation under Many Gods," October 2001, http://firstthings.com/article.php3?id_article=2234&var_recherche=eck (accessed January 12, 2008), and Stephen R. Prothero, *Religious Literacy: What Every American Needs to Know—and Doesn't* (New York: HarperOne, 2007), 33, 146. "U.S. Religious Landscape Survey: Affiliations," Pew Forum on Religion and Public Life, http://religions.pewforum.org/affiliations (accessed on January 12, 2008). Stephen R. Prothero, *The White Buddhist: The Asian Odyssey of Henry Steel Olcott* (Bloomington: Indiana University Press, 1996); and Richard Hughes Seager, *Buddhism in America* (New York: Columbia University Press, 2000). Thomas A. Tweed, *Our Lady of the Exile: Diasporic Religion at a Cuban Catholic Shrine in Miami* (New York: Oxford University Press, 2002); Robert A.

Orsi, *Thank You, St. Jude: Women's Devotion to the Patron Saint of Hopeless Causes* (New Haven: Yale University Press, 1998); and Karen McCarthy Brown, *Mama Lola, A Vodou Priestess in Brooklyn* (Berkeley: University of California Press, 2001).

19. Pew Forum on Religion and Public Life, "U.S. Religious Landscape Survey. Religious Affiliation: Diverse and Dynamic" (Washington, D.C.: Pew Forum on Religion and Public Life, 2008), 5, http://religions.pewforum.org/pdf/report-religious-landscape-study-full.pdf (accessed December 29, 2008).

PART 1

The State of American Religious History

Religious History in the Post-Ahlstrom Era

James M. O'Toole

In the winter of 2006 several graduate students in history at Boston College organized a conference on new approaches to the history of religion. They hatched the idea, solicited the papers, and managed the local arrangements. Over two days about fifty historians—from students to senior professors—presented their work on religion in various historical times and places. There were papers on the origins of the American Bible Belt, panels on feminism and religion in modern Britain, and much more. Because I am the dissertation advisor to the organizers, they asked me to provide some remarks at the concluding lunch. It seemed worthwhile, given the emphasis on new approaches to the subject, to look back and reflect on some older ones. This was not just the nostalgic impulse of a graying academic, fondly recalling the heady days of his own graduate-student youth. I thought it might be useful to draw some kind of baseline, a starting point from which to measure what had happened since and is happening now.

In 1972 Yale University Press published Sydney Ahlstrom's *Religious History of the American People.* Most American historians are familiar with it, though there are probably only a few of us who have actually read it cover to cover. It's a big book; it weighs just under five pounds. It is "synoptic"—an appropriate word, that—and its chronological scope is impressive. It opens with the Council of Constance (1418), which ended the Great Western Schism and reestablished the unity of European Christendom. The last chapter describes what Ahlstrom calls "the Turbulent Sixties"—the 1960s, that is, barely over as he was writing. Those recent years were a time, he said, not of consensus but of "dissensus" in religion as in other aspects of American life. There was a sharp break between the religious past and the religious present,

From *Historically Speaking* 8 (January/February 2007)

and the future did not seem particularly bright. "America's moral and religious tradition was tested and found wanting in the sixties," Ahlstrom concluded bluntly. Factors such as rapid technological change (the moon landing, for instance, only three years before), the disaffection of youth (Kent State University, two years earlier), changing roles for women in society (the Equal Rights Amendment, submitted to the states just as the book hit the stores)—all these and other social forces were challenging religion and the writing of its history.

Accordingly Ahlstrom took as his interpretive framework the idea that religion in America had had a remarkable consistency from the fifteenth century down to his own day. The nation might have been moving away from its earlier consensus, but that consensus had once been firmly in place, and it could be seen across the denominational lines. Through most of its history, America had been "the Protestant Empire," dominated in fact by a particular kind of Protestantism, the one associated with the independent Calvinist churches of early New England. Across the board religion in America had been "unmistakably conditioned by a Reformed and Puritan ethos." This ethos was gradually attenuated and secularized over time, but the country had nevertheless been "pervaded by an ideology which . . . was Puritan at the level of both personal and social ethics." Now, however, that ethos had unraveled, and what Ahlstrom called a "post-Protestant," even a "post-Puritan" era had arrived. This time of "post-"s threw into sharp relief the "pre-"s, and, standing as it did on that very cusp, Ahlstrom's book might serve as the earlier era's summary and capstone.

The reviewers all thought so, and they concluded that an older way of doing religious history had come to a close with the publication of Ahlstrom's *Religious History.* This book, they said, was a vast improvement over the largely denominational volumes of earlier scholars, but it was also the culmination of one way of approaching the subject. Jerald Brauer of the University of Chicago said in *Church History* that Ahlstrom's work was "probably the last and the very best of a long series of synthetic histories of the religious development of America. . . . It closes the door on one period and makes necessary the opening of doors to a new period of historiography." Henry Warner Bowden of Rutgers, reviewing the book for the *Journal of the American Academy of Religion,* compared Ahlstrom to Moses, no less: he brought scholars to a vantage point where they could see the "new terrain for future generations of students"—new topics to be explored, new methods to be tried—but he could not "cross over into that territory himself." No one, all the reviewers agreed, would ever write religious history quite this way again.

I remember reading some of these reviews when they first appeared, and it is interesting to go back and read them again now. In the intervening years my opinion has changed. At the time I thought the reviewers were simply wrong. "Whaddaya mean, religious history can't be written this way any more?" I said to myself. "Of course it can." For that matter, this was the only way to write the history of religion in America or anywhere else, wasn't it? You looked at the various religious institutions, their leadership, their theology. What laypeople did was too difficult to get at. And what, in any case, was historically significant about them? Religious history was inevitably a branch of intellectual history such as Ahlstrom had written. Perhaps no other scholar would be as comprehensive as he in the future, I thought, but he had correctly identified the story that was to be told, the phenomena that were to be analyzed. Paul Conkin of the University of Wisconsin seemed to confirm this position, even as he offered the most Waspish assessment in the pages of *Reviews in American History.* Conkin aimed his criticisms at Ahlstrom's supposed lack of what he called "dogmatic intellect," pointing out the book's failure to account adequately for the doctrinal differences between, say, Mormon and Adventist views of death and the afterlife. But Conkin's critique only reinforced the notion that dogma, the body of religious ideas, had to be at the heart of religious history.

Now I think the other reviewers were right after all. Broad as it is Ahlstrom's book does seem to offer a limited view, and its questions are no longer the only ones we want to ask. It is unappreciative at the least to take an eleven-hundred-page book, published three decades years ago, and point out all the things that aren't in it. But there are some obvious topics that get little or no treatment. Theologians and clergymen are the principal characters in the story, and these are, of course, overwhelmingly male. I did a rough count in the index: there are about twelve hundred personal-name entries, only about sixty of them women. This is an unfair criticism, but obviously no one could write about religion today and leave women out of the story. There are many other subjects that simply are not discussed. Even among the mainline Christian denominations there are lots of gaps. In the discussion of Methodism, for example, we necessarily meet the Wesley brothers. We are told of John's power as a preacher, but we never really hear much about the content of that preaching, why it had such an impact on people, or what they may have thought about it. The book is better on the post–Vatican II changes within Roman Catholicism (perhaps because they were more recent), but we still don't get an indication of how any of these were experienced by Catholics themselves. It is wrong, of course, to be Whiggish here, to blame Ahlstrom for not being like us. I bring all this up only to confirm the reviewers' opinions that this wonderful and essential book did indeed mark the end of a historiographical story. Since its publication, therefore, those of us who work in the history of religion have been living in what I call the post-Ahlstrom era.

What are the hallmarks of this period? Apart from the addition of previously overlooked religious traditions, the most significant development has been the advent of the "lived religion" approach. Historians now study religion as it was experienced and lived by laypeople. The landmark studies are familiar: Robert Orsi's *Madonna of 115th Street* (1985), Nancy Ammerman's *Bible Believers* (1987), David Hall's *Worlds of Wonder, Days of Judgment* (1989). On the European side John Bossy's *Christianity in the West* (1985) and Eamon Duffy's *Stripping of the Altars* (1992) and *Voices of Morebath* (2001) all show how religion might be approached from this perspective. It is from works such as these that we get Hall's "horse-shed Christians" (I always tell undergraduates that it's important to pronounce those words carefully), or Ammerman's "Golden Rule Christians," or, if I may say so, my own practitioners of "week-to-week" religion.

Many factors contributed to the success of this approach, none more so than the ways in which new sources were identified and used to study questions that had once seemed unanswerable. At least since Perry Miller in American history and giants like David Knowles in European history, the inevitable sources for religious historians were the writings of religious leaders and thinkers: sermons, doctrinal syntheses, official denominational statements, and so on. Just as other kinds of history were written from elite, primarily literate sources, so religious history relied on similar materials. The turn toward social history, however, just reaching full speed as Ahlstrom wrote, changed all that, and historians began to look for other sources, now recognized as chock-full of information about the experiences of regular people—in our case, those famously silent "men and women in the pews." Even those sources that had official, institutional origins contained details about nonofficial practices and beliefs. Churches run by male hierarchies were full of information about women, for instance, and about women's experiences. It might even be possible to find documentation of "things unseen," as the Christian scriptures call them.

Indulge me in a reference to my own work on the practice of confession among American Catholics in the nineteenth and twentieth centuries. Here was something done weekly and monthly by staggering numbers of ordinary parishioners, but it was conducted in secret; there are no records of what transpired. Trying to write such a history would be a foolish enterprise, you might say, or at least one to be undertaken only by someone who already has tenure. Why study a topic for which there is no evidence? But there is evidence: sermons and moral theology textbooks, yes; but also catechisms, pamphlets from the racks in the church vestibule, laypeople's letters to popular Catholic magazines, parish statistics, even parish weekly schedules that show the expansion and contraction of the hours set aside for this sacrament. By examining those and other sources, I've been able to see the extent to which average Catholics internalized their church's official teachings and made them their own—or not. Through a kind of inkblot switch, it's possible to use these apparently mundane sources to peel away the layers of lived religion.

In the process, I think, it has become easier to connect the history of religion to other areas of historical study, and this is a very positive development. Religious history has often seemed marginalized from other historical writing. Leslie Tentler of Catholic University tells of an Organization of American Historians' session in 1990 on "new directions" in Catholic history. "It's too bad," one member of the audience said in the discussion that followed the papers. "You folks do interesting work. But you'll always be marginal to the profession." The same might have been said to those who worked on religion elsewhere. Some of this marginalization was no doubt attributable to religious historians themselves, though there were other reasons for it, too. My own view (which I can't prove) is that the secularization of the academy and the people who pursue careers in it contributed to this as well. In any event, religion was reduced to Jon Butler's already-famous "jack-in-the-box" phenomenon. It popped up into view periodically—Prohibition and the Scopes Trial in the 1920s, politically active fundamentalism in the 1980s—but then it was stuffed back down into the box while other historical tunes began to play. By studying the religious experience of people who continued to go to church even when no one was watching (that is, while Jack was safely stowed inside the box), practitioners of the lived-religion approach could see how religion influenced and was influenced by other historical themes, including the reigning historiographical Holy Trinity: race, class, and gender. Work on black churches has been particularly successful at this, and the potential for studying religion through the lens of gender seems to me to be only now being realized. The questions to be asked aren't just about women and their religious experiences; they really are about gender as a category. Here is an opportunity for religious history to move decisively from the margins to the center.

This is all an encouraging sign of life for the history of religion. Religious historians have often felt that they get no respect—or not enough respect—

from their colleagues. But there is evidence that this is less so now than it was in the pre-Ahlstrom era. I was pleasantly surprised, for example, when I looked at the online directory of the American Historical Association, which lists about twenty-five thousand historians in universities and historical agencies in the United States and Canada. The directory allows AHA members to designate up to three topical fields of interest in addition to the particular country or time period they study. There are fifty possible subject choices, and one of them is religion. When I accessed the database last March [2005], 918 historians said that they worked on religion. This number was second only to the 1,014 who said they did "cultural" history, but if you add in the 237 historians who indicated that they did "Jewish" history (most of whom did not also check "religion"), religion is in first place.

So where does this leave us? The post-Ahlstrom era is now thirty years old, and no one can predict how long it might last. Historians will have to take account of new forms of religious diversity, particularly outside the West, both on their own terms and for the impact they have on more established groups. Levels of religious practice remain very high in America in comparison to other parts of the West, and history can help us understand this phenomenon. The future of the discipline is unknown, but it is clear that there is much work to do.

Beyond the Niebuhrs

An Interview with Robert Orsi on Recent Trends in American Religious History

Conducted by Randall J. Stephens

Robert Orsi is the Grace Craddock Nagle Chair in Catholic Studies in the religion department at Northwestern University; he holds a joint appointment in history. He taught at Harvard Divinity School from 2001 to 2007. Orsi's work on Catholic devotionalism and what some call "lived religion" has helped reorient religious history in the United States to the common men, women, and children who practice their faith from day to day. His *Between Heaven and Earth: The Religious Worlds People Make and the Scholars Who Study Them* (2005) combines autobiographical insight with keen scholarship. Peering into the worlds of devotees and academics, Orsi explores Catholic notions of suffering, the presence of the sacred for believers, and even scrutinizes serpent handlers and the observers who study them. He is currently completing a book on growing up Catholic in the twentieth-century United States. In that work he plans to explore the religious worlds children made and how they formed their beliefs in creative, imaginative ways. In May 2006 Randall Stephens, editor of *Historically Speaking*, spoke to Orsi in his office at Harvard University.

RANDALL STEPHENS: Would you comment on the concept of devotionalism that is so central to much of your work?

ROBERT ORSI: What intrigues me about devotionalism—and one of the reasons I find it so interesting and compelling to study historically—is that it's a charged field where institutional imperatives intersect with people's own

From *Historically Speaking* 7 (July/August 2006)

efforts and desires to engage the world religiously. There's a powerful interplay at work in devotional practice, and the results are not predictable. For instance, the cult of the Virgin Mary does not in any simple sense enforce a regime of docile femininity on living women. Women appropriate the Virgin Mary. They pray to her; they make her part of their lives. She becomes a mother, sister, grandmother to them, and as this happens, they use her to authorize their lives, to think about their lives in different ways, to make certain changes that might otherwise have been unthinkable. So I don't like the simple grid of empowerment/disempowerment. Devotionalism offers a much more subtle ground where people live real, necessarily limited, and contradictory lives.

STEPHENS: In *Thank You, St. Jude* you explore the combination of institutional and popular dynamics in Catholic devotionalism. You argue specifically that St. Jude became the patron saint of lost causes in part because devotional promoters in Chicago sold St. Jude to a mass audience. But there were also women who made the saint their own.

ORSI: I see this as the dialectic of devotionalism. Women didn't invent the devotions to St. Jude. The devotion was the creation of priests in Chicago who needed money for their new church in a poor Mexican neighborhood, and devotions were a rich source of income in the mid-twentieth century. So women inherited Jude. But once Jude was there, then women came and made Jude part of their lives, and in turn Jude helped them live these lives.

For example, the Catholic press in the 1930s and 1940s insisted that women not work outside the home, that the working mother was a bad mother. Yet, at the same time, women were praying to Jude in their devotions to him to help them find jobs because they needed to support their families. That's what I mean about devotionalism as the ground on which women could live their lives as they found them.

STEPHENS: Scholars like Eugene McCarraher have criticized the fusion of consumerism and Christianity in America. What are your thoughts on the subject?

ORSI: McCarraher is right. It's there all along. If you look back, for example, to Henry Ward Beecher's appearances in advertisements for soap and flour, you can see this at work, as well as in his sermons. Consumerist faith represented an effusive, romantic Christianity; modern Christians consumed to express and even to constitute their interiority. Modern American capitalism was able to make use of the religious cultures at its disposal and to transform them in the process.

STEPHENS: In a review of your latest book, *Between Heaven and Earth: The Religious Worlds People Make and the Scholars Who Study Them,* John T.

McGreevy criticizes your work for not giving enough credit to the bishops, priests, nuns, and lay leaders who changed the church after Vatican II in the 1960s. How do you respond?

ORSI: I don't think we have the historical materials yet to make generalizations about how the complex transformations of the era took hold or didn't. Take the trajectory of Reformation studies as an analogy here: understanding the processes of reform demanded town-by-town, if not street-by-street, studies. Something like this will be necessary to approach the effect of the Council's reforms, because there were regional variations, ethnic and social class variations, and so on. So local studies of how things developed after the Second Vatican Council—the liturgical changes, ethical rethinking, the serious theological reformulations the Council offered—are still necessary. We need some account of how these matters were presented to laity in different parts of the country by different clergies. The Midwestern experience of the era was different, for instance, from that in the old industrial Northeast. We're not at a place yet to make generalizations about the reception of the Second Vatican Council.

Having said that, I've been doing soundings in local history as I research my book on growing up Catholic in the twentieth century. Again, as in past work, I've been using ethnography as well as history, and the people I've spoken to around the country in what I've been calling memory groups have very much wanted to talk about their experience before and after the Council. Time after time I was told that church officials presented the mandated liturgical and ecclesiastical changes without explanation, without discussion among laypeople. I haven't heard of any instances where pastors held public conversations to explain, "these are the changes, let's talk about our feelings about the changes, and our understandings." This was not the culture of Catholicism at that time. Priests were not inclined or trained to go out to the laity and say, "You know, the Friday meat prohibition is now being lifted. Let's talk about what you think about that and what you feel." Vatican II and its aftermath represented the changing nature of Catholicism in the United States and worldwide. It marked a deep revolution in how people experienced their sacred world. Its history remains to be told.

STEPHENS: How well do you think American religious historians understand the American religious experience in general?

ORSI: American religious history, as it is practiced in the universities today, is insistently committed, consciously or not, to Niebuhrian neo-orthodoxy as its moral vision, and this profoundly influences the historiography. We celebrate those aspects of American religious history that are admirable from the neo-orthodox perspective. We don't even ask, "Was the rise of neo-orthodoxy a good thing?" It's arguable that as mainline Protestant seminaries in the U.S. became neo-orthodox strongholds, as they almost all did, obsessed with the idea that Christian integrity demanded a Christ against culture, Protestant liberal clergy lost the capacity effectively to participate in and to speak to American culture. Was this a good thing? But neo-orthodoxy as a lens for American religious historiography prevents us from asking these kinds of questions. There are exceptions—I think of Marie Griffith's work on Christian diets or Larry Moore's study of Christian entertainments, and so on, studies done without the edge of moral condemnation that otherwise so characterizes the field.

Beyond that, how much does neo-orthodoxy or Niebuhrian realism tell us about American religion? I tell my students that if they want to understand the history of modern American religion, they have to look at figures like Henry Ward Beecher and Norman Vincent Peale. I say this without then going on to impose a neo-orthodox moral judgment on such figures. Beecher is more important than the figures we tend to lionize because, in fact, American Christianity became his Christianity.

STEPHENS: There are some in the field who have turned attention to other areas. One thinks of historians like George Marsden, Mark Noll, and Nathan Hatch, for example. Marsden has also called historians who happen to be Christian to acknowledge or embrace their faith perspectives. He has argued that religious viewpoints "ought to be granted a fully legitimate place in the mainstream academy so long as they prove themselves academically worthy in the same way that other points of view do."[1] Would you agree with him?

ORSI: As much as I respect his work, I've never quite understood what George Marsden is talking about when he criticizes the allegedly exclusive secularity of the American university. First of all there's no lack of respect for evangelical historians in the academy. He himself is surely proof of that. And this is true of all the historians who are in the evangelical circle: Mark Noll, Joel Carpenter, Grant Wacker, among others. I don't see any exclusion of these historians from any conversation on the grounds of their personal commitments. So, too, Richard Bushman is a distinguished and widely admired Mormon scholar of Mormonism. It strikes me that there's a little bit of the "evangelical as victim" thing going on here. But I don't think there's any truth to such claims. If a historian does his or her work well, I truly don't see what the issue is.

When I had just gotten out of graduate school and was in my first teaching job, I was given the unhappy but necessary assignment of speaking with an evangelical Ph.D. student who wanted to argue that the unpredictability of the first Great Awakening, its odd patterns and surprising conversions, pointed to the reality that the Holy Spirit was the cause of the revival. I had to tell him that this was an unacceptable interpretation, and if he persisted. he wouldn't be allowed to continue in the program. Now if this is what evangelical critics are talking about, if that's what it means to bring one's religious vision into the classroom, then I think this position is completely inappropriate. You can't get an academic degree based on notions of divine causality given that our critical inquiry is necessarily limited to the human. But I don't think this is what they mean.

If the argument of the evangelical critique is that we need to give a rich and nuanced account of people's religious worlds, of their religious thought, and of the religious motivations that move them—move them even apart from political or economic considerations—I can't think of a single American religious historian who would dissent. So Marsden's argument strikes me as criticism without an object in view.

STEPHENS: What do you make of Stanley Hauerwas's claim that religious studies departments make campuses inhospitable for people who practice their faith?

ORSI: I find it tendentious. I have yet to see any evidence for this, and surely such statements, to be acceptable in a university, require evidence. Religious studies departments—and I am familiar with many of them—are venues for the careful, attentive, and critical study of different religions. I have never heard of a student's religious question being rudely dismissed in a classroom. It is the case that critical studies of religion raise questions about religious worlds that might make some practitioners uncomfortable. But professors are generally quite willing to talk about even this discomfort in classrooms or in office hours. Is Hauerwas calling for a faith that is not up to intellectual scrutiny? Clearly not, given his work in general. Again I don't get the point of such critical attacks.

STEPHENS: I believe his point is that the pluralism of the academy doesn't make room for people who are exclusivist.

ORSI: But what does this mean in practice? If people are exclusivists and think that Hinduism is the devil's work, would that mean they would or should dismiss the study of that subject, that they could go into a classroom and teach Hinduism as demonic or wrong or inadequate because Hindus don't acknowledge Jesus as lord and savior? How would this advance knowledge? On the other hand plenty of foundational work in the study of religions other than Christianity was done by deeply committed and exclusivist Christians. The question is how Christians deal responsibly with their Christianity in an environment of open critical inquiry, in which all questions are fair game. And regardless of what some evangelicals say, the same is asked of all professors, whatever their personal commitments.

A photographer friend of mine, Rich Remsberg, produced a fine book of photos and text on Pentecostal motorcycle riders called *Riders for God.* I got to visit the bikers' church a few times with Rich. This was in rural southern Indiana. The pastor came over to me one night during a little conversation hour after one of the services and asked, "So what do you do?" I told him that I was the chair of the religious studies department at Indiana University. "Well, what do you teach there?" he wanted to know. I said, "We teach all the world religions, Christianity, Hinduism, Buddhism, and so on." And he teased me, although he was serious, "You teach those other religions to show how they're wrong, right? How Christianity is the only true religion?" That's okay for a church but not for a university.

STEPHENS: In *Between Heaven and Earth* you remark that it is a challenge to write about figures of "special power"—saints, demons, ancestors, gods, ghosts—as agents in history. Could you elaborate on how you go about that?

ORSI: I think that the religious studies community does a pretty good job of thinking about these questions. Dipesh Chakrabarty's *Provincializing Europe: Postcolonial Thought and Historical Difference* [2000] issues a strong challenge from subaltern studies to the historical guild, asking us to think about how such supernatural figures held so closely by various peoples act in history. I think religious historians have done a better job of writing about angels, demons, spirits, et cetera, especially when they're not looking over their shoulders apprehensively at what secular historians might say about this. It's important to see the ways in which figures like St. Jude are not puppets being manipulated by the clergy or by women. They are, in fact, rich imaginative creations that acquire a vivid life of their own and in an important and historically relevant sense break free of their creators.

STEPHENS: Certainly, someone who is devout would say, "These are not 'creations.' They're independent beings that exist in their own right."

ORSI: I'm really interested in the question of *how* these figures become real in particular times and places. My current work helps me understand how children relate to these figures, and this in turn is helping me find ways of thinking about historical and cultural reality, since the cast of a culture's imagination begins in its work with children. How do the apparitions at Lourdes or the religious manifestations at the 1906 Pentecostal revival on Azusa Street in Los Angeles become real for devotees? Or what historical sense can be made of the fact that people claimed to see Jesus during one of Aimee Semple McPherson's revivals? Do we fall back on crude notions of mass hysteria, or can we learn to think differently about such historical realities? For the faithful there's something ontologically unsurprising going on. But how can we historians talk about the human historical and cultural dimensions of such things?

STEPHENS: What drew you to the topic of children?

ORSI: Historian Steven Mintz writes that children are largely invisible in history. They're doubly invisible in religious history. Often they show up in religious contexts as objects of adult dread and fear. Periodically in American religious history there have been moments of high anxiety about the risks that the culture is posing to children, the dangers of American life to children, or the dangers that children are posing to society. And there are certain incidents that could easily be recast as children's events, like the colonial revivals in which children were active, indeed initial, participants. As I write in my book, all the Marian apparitions of the nineteenth and early twentieth centuries were to children. Still children have been really invisible in American religious history and in religious history generally. So this challenge drew me. But in terms of American Catholicism, which throughout the twentieth century was not only preoccupied with the religious formation of children but had built one of the most extensive institutional structures to achieve this, it is impossible to understand the life of the modern Catholic church in the U.S. without understanding it as the creation of adults and children in relation to each other.

STEPHENS: In the religious communities you study how have adults understood children and childhood?

ORSI: I think part of the problem is that adult-children relations in religious settings have not been approached with the full complexity and historical specificity that they require. There's the idea that adults *pass on* their religious beliefs to children, but this is always a fraught process, the "passing on." That's particularly the case if we're talking about immigrant families or migrant families. I wrote an article many years ago in the *Journal of Social History* about the "religious fault lines" that I saw between southern Italian immigrants and their American children, and the question has been on my mind since. To what extent has modern American Catholicism been shaped by this particular fault line? But there are real problems with finding children in history. You have to use a historical methodology akin to that of historians using Inquisitional documents to reach the lives of the people the Inquisition targeted and who appear in documents refracted through authority. I have been using in part works written for or about children by adults, including prescriptive literature and Catholic children's comics.

STEPHENS: It sounds like the problem of using European colonial sources to study Native Americans.

ORSI: Right. You're reading Jesuit mission documents to understand Native American religious cultures. That's why I've been using memory groups around the country, getting groups of people together in different parts of the U.S. I've been talking to people over fifty about their memories of growing up and what their childhoods were like and then setting those memories in relationship to whatever printed sources I can find.

STEPHENS: What is your impression of the religious worlds that these children created or inhabited in pre–Vatican II America?

ORSI: One way of approaching the history of a particular culture of childhood is to begin with the anomalous, for instance with a story that you can't imagine a nun actually telling or a religious idea that is completely idiosyncratic. For example I came across a widespread children's notion that God made priests forget everything that they just heard in confession. Kids made that up some place at some time, working with what the nuns told them about the seal of the confessional. They told this to each other. So this idea becomes an item for historical reflection, raising the question, What was it that children were so concerned about that caused them to generate this story? What does it disclose about children's fears, desires, and their experience of the confessional?

STEPHENS: How will your work on the subject expand our knowledge of American religious history in general?

ORSI: I agree that that's a question a historian of childhood has to ask. How does this contribute to the general historiography? To take one example there was real pressure on American priests from the 1920s forward to be able to speak to children, to be able to address children in language they could understand, in part because there were so many children around, because Catholics insisted that their children go to church from a very early age. Priests became specialists in "boyology," and particular priests developed reputations, in some cases nationally, as being good with boys. Modern Catholic notions of clerical deportment, in other words, the style and delivery of clerical authority, developed in part in relation with children. Putting children back in the picture raises suggestive questions about the actual making of lived religious worlds and about adult lives.

Note

1. George Marsden, "Christian Advocacy and the Rules of the Academic Game," in *Religious Advocacy and American History,* ed. Bruce Kuklick and D. G. Hart (Grand Rapids, Mich.: Eerdmans, 1997), 7.

Religion in American History

An Interview with Stephen Prothero

Conducted by Randall J. Stephens

Stephen Prothero's *Religious Literacy: What Every American Needs to Know—and Doesn't* (2007) calls for renewed commitment to religious education. A *New York Times* bestseller, the book is a forceful critique of the growing ignorance of religion and religious history. U.S. citizens are markedly more religious than their secular European counterparts. Yet, unlike Europeans, Americans know very little about ancient and modern religions that have shaped the East and the West. Professor of religion at Boston University, Prothero has authored a number of other books and articles on American religious history. Editor of *Historically Speaking* Randall Stephens spoke with Prothero about his work and the state of the field in November 2007.

RANDALL STEPHENS: How has the field of American religious history changed in the last few decades?

STEPHEN PROTHERO: Ethnography has dominated religious history since the 1980s. Robert Orsi's *Madonna of 115th Street: Faith and Community in Italian Harlem, 1880–1950* [1985] had a major impact. Scholars started teaching that and Karen McCarthy Brown's *Mama Lola: A Vodou Priestess in Brooklyn* [1991]. Then Thomas Tweed wrote the influential *Our Lady of the Exile: Diasporic Religion at a Cuban Catholic Shrine in Miami* [1997]. About five years ago I looked at a number of syllabi for American religion courses, and I noticed a shift away from metanarrative to ethnographic studies, which often have a historical component.

From *Historically Speaking* 9 (May/June 2008)

STEPHENS: How then does Mark Noll's sprawling history *America's God: From Jonathan Edwards to Abraham Lincoln* [2002] fit into the field?

PROTHERO: It doesn't fit. And one of the things that intrigues me is that evangelicals are more willing to do metanarratives. I've wondered why. Is it because they live inside metanarratives or perhaps because they're not as tied into the fads of the profession?

STEPHENS: Is there a sharp division in religious studies between those who rely heavily on theory and those who don't?

PROTHERO: Those who do American religious history come at it either from the history profession or religious studies. The latter are trying to tell you something about religion in America, but they're also trying to tell you something about religion in general. And I think that's where theory comes in. If you look at the journal *Religion in American Culture,* the articles always include some theory. In other words it's not enough to tell a story and provide an explanation. You have to make some broader connections, so that somebody who does Hinduism in India can read the article and think, "Oh that's interesting, what they did with twentieth-century Pentecostalism." A religious historian from the history side, like Yale's Harry Stout, does not operate with the same set of questions and constraints. Historians seem classically allergic to theory.

STEPHENS: Are there other concerns that shape how religious studies scholars work?

PROTHERO: We don't really have a discipline like historians do, so we're always ripping things off from other people. Religious studies still has a lingering status-anxiety problem. It has had to justify itself. That's less the case since 9/11. Obviously it's harder for administrators to ask the stupid question "Why should we study religion?" I discuss this in my book *Religious Literacy: What Every American Needs to Know—and Doesn't* [2007]. Not long ago I spoke on the subject at the University of Florida. Religious studies students asked, "Why don't you do more with Judaism?" And my answer was, "Because it doesn't matter as much. It doesn't have the same influence that Christianity did and does." That was a historian's answer. I wrote more about Christianity in *Religious Literacy,* because 85 percent of Americans are Christian, because all the presidents have been Christian, and because Christianity is the language of American politics.

I think about the issue of content and emphasis in terms of the courses I teach. In my American religion class I talk about the various efforts to come up with a religious character of America. It's a Protestant nation. It's a Christian nation. It's a Judeo-Christian nation. It's a Judeo-Christian-Islamic nation. The idea of a religiously united country has a history. But then there is another image, which Diana Eck lays out in *A New Religious America: How a "Christian Country" Has Become the World's Most Religiously Diverse Nation* [2001]: we're secular by law, pluralistic in reality. So there's a tension between the two, between the unitive impulse and the more pluralistic impulse. The unitive impulse keeps getting broader. After 9/11 it went to the Judeo-Christian-Islamic idea. That was an interesting conversation: "Are we Judeo-Christian-Islamic, or are we multicultural?" The Hindus got in there and sent a letter to George Bush that asked, "Why aren't we at the interfaith gatherings? Why is it that Christians, Jews, and Muslims define the nation religiously?" I occasionally ask my students at Boston University, "Is the United States a Christian country?" The Christians always say no, and the Jews always say yes. The Jews tend to reply, "Are you kidding me? Of course it's a Christian country. I feel that every day, I have the sense every day that this is a Christian place where we get Christmas off, but we don't get Passover off."

STEPHENS: One of the reasons my American religious history students liked your book *American Jesus: How the Son of God Became a National Icon* [2003] was because it shows so much change over time. It's primarily a work of history.

PROTHERO: A religious studies treatment of the topic would have been more synchronic. The tension between history and religious studies is essentially between anthropology and history.

STEPHENS: What drew you to the study of religious history?

PROTHERO: Ever since I was young I was interested in religion. In college I just met a lot of different people who had a lot of different religious perspectives—friends who were atheists, friends who were Jewish, friends who were secularists. I had a kind of crisis of faith in college, actually. I was studying religion and politics, and I took a course with Richard Wightman Fox in American history. From high school I thought that history was the most boring subject imaginable. In fact when I went to Yale, I said I was going to take every subject except for history. Memorizing dates and names did not appeal to me. Richard taught me that history is as much about argument as it is about the past, which to me was exciting. And so I debated with others about views of the past.

I entered the field through a combination of losing my faith, being interested in religious questions, and then finding history as a way to ask those religious questions without the assumption that I had some great answer to the theological questions.

STEPHENS: Have you encountered any opposition from religious groups or devotees who feel that they have been misrepresented in your work?

PROTHERO: Well there has always been that sort of battle between the historian and the believer. After I wrote *American Jesus,* I was eager to hear what evangelicals would say about it. In some ways the book is addressed to evangelicals; at least it has a polemic there. It has a number of polemics, but I think one of them is that I haven't found a Jesus in America that isn't American. Quite a few evangelicals I spoke to commented, "The book has really made me question to what extent my faith is really Biblical and to what extent my faith is a product of American culture. I don't want it to be simply a product of American culture so I'm going to go back and check and make sure that what I believe is really based on the Bible." Quite a few others wrote, "I was really chastened because I realized that a lot of my views of Jesus came from the 1960s." I received very few letters along the lines of, "You should know that the real Jesus is . . ."

STEPHENS: Why is it that history courses on post–Civil War America seldom cover religious topics?

PROTHERO: Because academics are secularists. And I think we all have the tendency to extrapolate from our own experience. So you have a bunch of professors at Harvard or Princeton who aren't moved by religion, and they find it hard to imagine anyone else who is. The academy, the law, and the media are the three strangely secular areas of American culture. As such academics have largely misunderstood fundamentalism. I praise fundamentalists for being intellectuals in *Religious Literacy.* They have taken religious thought seriously. There are so many stereotypes of fundamentalists, and one is that they read the Bible literally. That's ridiculous. How do you read a text like Revelation literally?

STEPHENS: Your work on representations of Jesus through American history sheds light on believers across the spectrum. What do depictions of Jesus over the last one hundred years tell us about the American religious scene?

PROTHERO: For many Jesus became detached from the Bible. Visually Jesus was once portrayed in the context of Bible stories. In *American Jesus* I included images of Jesus stilling the storm, walking on water, or Jesus on the cross. But the images that appeared after Warner Sallman painted his iconic bust of Jesus were markedly different. These new images were not narrative and were not drawn from the Bible.

STEPHENS: It's literally disembodied.

PROTHERO: It's only a headshot, but it's also utterly outside of narrative and outside of scripture. It is the visual representation of the shift from knowing Jesus to loving Jesus. What matters now is loving him, and you can love him without knowing him.

STEPHENS: Something similar has happened as evangelicals stopped singing hymns steeped in theology and started singing simple choruses or love songs to Jesus.

PROTHERO: Religious literacy involves doctrinal and narrative knowledge. One should know the Bible stories and the teachings of the church. Both of those have been replaced by an experiential engagement with Jesus. That's one feature of American evangelicalism.

STEPHENS: And another aspect of evangelicalism centers on morality?

PROTHERO: It's a morality of the bedrooms. Though when I read the Bible, I don't see a preoccupation with that.

STEPHENS: Why since the 1960s have certain moral issues preoccupied conservative Christians in America?

PROTHERO: I think it's because the religious Right defined itself against the counterculture. The counterculture as defined by rock music and sexual permissiveness received special attention. Much of what conservative evangelicals saw in the 1960s had to do with sexuality: the emergence of sexuality in the public sphere, the acceptance of homosexuality, rising divorce rates, premarital sex, and the pill.

STEPHENS: There is a generational component here, right? Are younger evangelicals as motivated by some of these issues as their parents were?

PROTHERO: In 2002 Penny Long Marler and C. Kirk Hadaway published a study that investigated the shift among young people into the spiritual-but-not-religious demographic.[1] According to polls some people associated being religious with being right wing. So part of what the authors were saying wasn't just that younger Americans didn't like institutional religion; they also didn't like George Bush. In American history we've had the sense that religion is somehow alive in a particular approach to politics. The success of the Republicans in lining up with the religious Right has created an interesting climate. In some cases it has created an opening for people who want to get out of religion in the same way that Europeans have done so. Now the religious Left is trying to get the Democratic Party to strike a religious pose. It makes one wonder whether Americans will be fed up with that approach as well. If Americans see religion as a bulwark for intolerant partisans, they may become jaded.

STEPHENS: Does knowledge of other religions lead to understanding or tolerance?

PROTHERO: In *Religious Literacy* I intentionally resisted a sort of happy liberal approach that holds that the more we learn about other religions, the more we're going to get along. I say in the book that sometimes you want to kill someone because you don't know anything about them, sometimes you want to kill them because you know quite well who they are. So I don't think religious literacy is a kind of magic bullet to the problem of intolerance.

STEPHENS: What are you working on now?

PROTHERO: My next book project is a world religion textbook. Some readers of *Religious Literacy* seemed to be saying, "Give me religious literacy." I modeled that book on E. D. Hirsch's *Cultural Literacy: What Every American Needs to Know* [1988]. But unlike Hirsch, who only included a list of undefined items in the back of his book, I put a dictionary in the back of my book and a religious literacy quiz. Hirsch was criticized because his list was too narrow.

STEPHENS: When asked why he didn't include Cinco de Mayo on his list, Hirsch drew a blank and famously commented, "I'm afraid I don't know what that is."

PROTHERO: Hence there were larger criticisms of a narrowly white male view of what mattered. In addition Hirsch didn't even try to tell you what "Achilles' heel" meant. He just put it on his list. I thought I wanted to provide some content to religious literacy. Still a number of readers remarked, "I wish there was more. I wish you had told me more about the world's religions." So I am going to do a book on world religions that tries to be a basic religious literacy text.

Note

1. Penny Long Marler and C. Kirk Hadaway, "'Being Religious' or 'Being Spiritual' in America: A Zero-Sum Proposition?" *Journal for the Scientific Study of Religion* 41 (June 2002): 289–300.

PART 2

Judaism and Catholicism

The Challenges of Assimilation

American Judaism in Historical Perspective

Jonathan D. Sarna

Thirty years ago, when I mentioned my interest in American Jewish history to a scholar at a distinguished rabbinical seminary, he was absolutely appalled. "American Jewish history," he growled, "I'll tell you all that you need to know about American Jewish history: The Jews came to America, they abandoned their faith, they began to live like *goyim,* and after a generation or two they intermarried and disappeared. That is American Jewish history; all the rest is commentary. Don't waste your time. Go and study Talmud."

Many readers surely recognize this assimilationist paradigm. It is a close cousin to the secularization thesis that once held sway in the study of religion. In American Judaism it might be called "the myth of linear descent," the belief that American Jews start off Orthodox, back in the immigrant generation, and each subsequent generation is a little less Jewish in its observance until that inevitable day when a descendant intermarries and ends up marching down the aisle of a church. Actively by choice or passively through inaction, assimilation has been widely assumed to be unavoidable. My field of American Jewish history, if not a complete waste of time, is viewed as a foredoomed enterprise.

Yet the history of American Judaism, at least as I have come to understand it in writing my *American Judaism: A History* (2004), is in many ways a response to this ongoing fear that Judaism in the New World will wither away. Over and over again I found Jews rising to meet the challenges both internal and external that threatened Jewish continuity, sometimes, paradoxically, by promoting radical discontinuities. Casting aside old paradigms Jews transformed their faith, reinventing American Judaism in an attempt to make it more appealing, more meaningful, and more sensitive to the concerns of the day. They did not always succeed, as the many well-publicized accounts of

From *Historically Speaking* 5 (May/June 2004)

eminent Christians whose parents, grandparents, or great-grandparents turn out to have been Jews amply attest. But the story of American Judaism, at least as I recount it, is still far from the stereotypical story of "linear descent." It is, instead, a much more stereotypical story of people struggling to be Americans and Jews, a story of people who lose their faith and a story of people who regain their faith, a story of assimilation, to be sure, but also a story of revitalization.

In the 1820s some highly motivated and creative young Jews in the two largest American communities where Jews lived, New York and Charleston, moved to transform and revitalize their faith, somewhat in the spirit of the contemporaneous Second Great Awakening. They hoped, in so doing, to thwart Christian missionaries who insisted that in order to be modern one had to be Protestant, and they sought most of all to bring Jews back to active observance of their faith. They were alarmed by the spirit of Jewish "apathy and neglect" they discerned all around them.

The young people in New York "gathering with renewed arduor [*sic*] to promote the more strict keeping of their faith"[1] formed an independent society entitled Hebra Hinuch Nearim, dedicated to the education of Jewish young people. Their constitution and by-laws bespeak their spirit of revival, expressing "an ardent desire to promote the study of our Holy Law, and . . . to extend a knowledge of its divine precepts, ceremonies, and worship among our brethren generally, and the enquiring youth in particular." Worship, they insisted, should be run much less formally, with time set aside for explanations and instruction, without a permanent leader and, revealingly, with no "distinctions" made among the members. The overall aim, leaders explained in an 1825 letter, was "to encrease [*sic*] the respect of the worship of our fathers."[2]

In these endeavors we see all of the themes familiar to us from the general history of American religion, not only in that era but in many other eras of religious change including our own: revivalism, challenge to authority, a new form of organization, antielitism, and radical democratization. Given the spirit of the age and the fortunate availability of funding, it comes as no surprise that the young people plunged ahead, boldly announcing "their intention to erect a new Synagogue in this city," that would follow the "German and Polish minhag [rite]" and be located "in a more convenient situation for those residing uptown."[3] On November 15 the new congregation applied for incorporation as B'nai Jeshurun, New York's first Ashkenazic congregation.[4]

In Charleston, where a far better known schism within the Jewish community occurred, one finds several close parallels to the New York situation.

Again the challenge came initially from young Jews, born after the Revolution. Their average age was about thirty-two, while the average age of the leaders of Charleston's Beth Elohim congregation approached sixty-two. Dissatisfied with "the apathy and neglect which have been manifested towards our holy religion," somewhat influenced by the spread of Unitarianism in Charleston, fearful of Christian missionary activities that had begun to be directed toward local Jews, and, above all, like their New York counterparts, passionately concerned about Jewish survival, forty-seven men petitioned congregational leaders to break with tradition and institute change.[5]

The Charleston reformers were about two-thirds, native born, and most were people of comparatively modest means who participated in local civic affairs. According to one account, almost three-quarters of them were not paying members of the synagogue. In Charleston, as so often in the history of American Judaism, change was stimulated by outsiders. The changes that the reformers sought to effect, moreover, were far more radical than anything that had been called for in New York. They advocated, among other things, an abbreviated service, vernacular prayers, a weekly sermon, and an end to traditional free-will offerings in the synagogue. When their petition was dismissed out of hand, they, anticipating the New Yorkers by several months, created an independent Jewish religious society, "The Reformed Society of Israelites for Promoting True Principles of Judaism According to its Purity and Spirit"—a forerunner of American Reform Judaism.[6]

The 1820s marked the first revitalization of Judaism that I know of in America. But it was certainly not the last. Late-nineteenth-century America witnessed an immensely influential Jewish awakening. This revival was spawned not by East European Jews but by American-born Jews—most of whom traced their roots to German-speaking Central Europe—who were alarmed at evidence of assimilation in American Jewish life: religious laxity, intermarriage, interest in ethical culture, and the like. Spurred also by the growth of anti-Semitism in this era, they created what they called alternately a "revival," an "awakening," and a "renaissance."[7] This late-nineteenth-century awakening does not fit into the standard paradigm of American Jewish history. Central European Jews, all of us were taught, assimilated out of existence: how, then, could they have staged a revival? Rather than exploring this paradox (or altering the paradigm), most accounts of American Jewish life simply ignore these developments altogether and focus on East European Jewish immigration instead.

For me, however, the late-nineteenth-century awakening illustrates a major theme in American Judaism: the fact that repeatedly, down to our very own day, American Jews have creatively *adapted* their faith to their new environment. Reshaping Judaism in response to challenges from within and from without, they have time and again revitalized their faith, strengthening it, sometimes in surprising and unexpected ways that have brought Jews back into synagogues and produced children more religiously knowledgeable and observant than their parents. The fear that Judaism would not survive unless it changed certainly underlay many of these developments. But, in retrospect, the many creative responses to this fear, the innovations and revivals promoted by those determined to ensure that American Jewish life would continue and thrive, seem to me of far greater historical significance.

Another central theme of the history of American Judaism is the fact that for the major part of American history, Judaism has been the nation's largest and most visible non-Christian faith. Every Jew, every synagogue, every Jewish organization, periodical, and philanthropy has served as a conspicuous challenge to those who sought to define the nation (or its soul) in restrictively Christian terms.

From their very first steps on American soil, back in 1654, Jews extended the boundaries of American pluralism, serving as a model for other religious minorities and, in time, expanding the definition of American religious liberty so that they (and other minorities) might be included as equals. Recall that Peter Stuyvesant, the dictatorial director-general of New Netherland and himself an elder of the Reformed Church and the son of a minister, sought to compel the Jews to depart. His mission was to establish order among the citizenry, to combat "drinking to excess, quarreling, fighting and smiting." Seeking to promote morality and social cohesion, he looked to enforce Calvinist orthodoxy while rooting out nonconformity.[8]

This explains why Stuyvesant sought permission from Amsterdam to keep the Jews out. The Jews, he explained, were "deceitful," "very repugnant," and "hateful enemies and blasphemers of the name of Christ." He asked the directors of the Dutch West India Company to "require them in a friendly way to depart" lest they "infect and trouble this new colony." Revealingly he warned in a subsequent letter that in "giving them liberty we cannot refuse the Lutherans and Papists." Decisions made concerning the Jews, he understood, would serve as precedents and determine the colony's religious character forever after.[9]

Largely for economic reasons (as well as the fact that Jews numbered among its principal shareholders), the Dutch West India Company turned Peter Stuyvesant's plea down. They ordered him to permit Jews to "travel," "trade," "live," and "remain" in New Netherland, "provided the poor among them shall not become a burden to the company or to the community, but be supported by their own nation." After several more petitions, Jews secured the right to trade throughout the colony, serve guard duty, and own real estate. They also won the right to worship in the privacy of their homes, which, according to some accounts, is more than the Lutherans were permitted to do.[10]

This opening of the colony to Jews, just as Stuyvesant feared, soon determined policy for members of the colony's other minority faiths as well. "We doubt very much whether we can proceed against [these faiths] rigorously without diminishing the population and stopping immigration which must be favored at so tender stage of the country's existence," the directors admonished in 1663 after Stuyvesant banished a Quaker from the colony and spoke out against "sectarians." "You may therefore shut your eyes, at least not force people's consciences, but allow every one to have his own belief, as long as he behaves quietly and legally, gives no offense to his neighbor and does not oppose the government."[11] Under the British, who took New Amsterdam in 1664 and renamed it New York, this policy was maintained. In the 1740s the city boasted houses of worship for Anglicans, Dutch Calvinists, French Huguenots, German Lutherans, Presbyterians, Baptists, Quakers, and Jews.

After the American Revolution Jews once again played a role in ensuring that religious liberty was not restricted to Christians alone sometimes, as in New York, simply by being present. It is probably no accident that New York, the most religiously pluralistic of the new states, was the first to grant "free exercise and enjoyment of religious profession and worship, without discrimination or preference" to all its citizens, Christian and non-Christian alike. Pennsylvania's new constitution was more restrictive, requiring officeholders to "acknowledge the Scriptures of the old and new Testament to be given by divine inspiration." But after several widely publicized petitions from Jews, that clause was dropped in 1790. The United States Constitution, of course, followed the most liberal state precedents, and thanks to Charles Pinckney of South Carolina (another state with a visible Jewish community), it explicitly included the words "no religious test shall ever be required as a qualification to any office or public trust under the authority of the United States." Revealingly the only petition concerning religious liberty that reached the federal Constitutional Convention also came from a Jew, Jonas Phillips, who memorably declared that "the Israeletes will think them self happy to live under a government where all Relegious societys are on an Eaquel footing."[12]

The famed correspondence between Jews and George Washington went even further in defining the place of Judaism in the new nation. The address of the "Hebrew Congregation in Newport" to the president, composed for his visit to that city on August 17, 1790, following Rhode Island's ratification of the Constitution, paralleled other letters that Washington received from religious bodies of different denominations and followed a long-established custom associated with the ascension of kings. Redolent with biblical and liturgical language, the address noted past discrimination against Jews, praised the new government for "generously affording to all liberty of conscience and immunities of citizenship," and thanked God "for all of the blessings of civil and religious liberty" that Jews now enjoyed under the Constitution. Washington, in his oft-quoted reply, reassured the Jewish community about what he correctly saw as its central concern—religious liberty. Appropriating a phrase contained in the Hebrew congregation's original letter, he characterized the United States government as one that "gives to bigotry no sanction, to persecution no assistance." He described religious liberty, following Thomas Jefferson, as an inherent natural right, distinct from the indulgent religious "toleration" practiced by the British and much of enlightened Europe, where Jewish emancipation was so often linked with demands for Jewish "improvement." Finally echoing the language of the prophet Micah (4:4), he hinted that America might itself prove something of a Promised Land for Jews, a place where they would "merit and enjoy the good will of the other inhabitants; while everyone shall sit in safety under his own vine and fig tree and there shall be none to make him afraid."[13]

Diversity is the third theme in the history of American Judaism and one, to my mind, that has been absolutely central almost from the very beginning. In the seventeenth and eighteenth centuries every known colonial American Jewish community included both Sephardim and Ashkenazim and comprised Jews who came from widely scattered backgrounds. By 1790 the United States census recorded Jews who had been born in England, France, Germany, Holland, Poland, Portugal, and the West Indies, as well as in the American colonies, a mix that mirrored the composition of the late colonial Jewish community as well.[14] The Sephardic form of Judaism predominated, as it always had in North America, but from the early eighteenth century onward most colonial Jews were actually Ashkenazim or people of mixed background. Within every community, even within many individual families, a full gamut of religious observances and attitudes could be found, a spectrum ranging all the way from deep piety to total indifference. In the years following the American Revolution, Jacob Rader Marcus found that "there were almost as many Judaisms as there were individuals."[15] In matters of religious practice, as in so many other aspects of life during the early republic, individual freedom reigned supreme, setting a pattern that would govern American Jewish life forever after.

Jewish life in America became even more diverse following the migration of tens of thousands of Central European Jews from Bavaria, Western Prussia, Poland, and Alsace between 1820 and 1880. During that time America's Jewish population ballooned from about 3,000 to around 250,000. Immigrants spread out across the length and breadth of the country, reaching all the way to California. Already by the Civil War the number of organized Jewish communities with at least one established Jewish institution had reached 160, distributed over thirty-one states and the District of Columbia. Jews moved into every region of the country and lived in more than a thousand other American locations during this period, wherever rivers, roads, or railroad tracks took them. Like the bulk of immigrants to America's shores, then and later, they pursued opportunities wherever they found them.[16]

During this era the diversity of American Jewish life was often reflected in the diversity of American synagogues, each committed to a different *minhag,* or rite, such as the German rite, the Polish rite, the English rite, and so forth. By the Civil War, every major American Jewish community had at least two synagogues, and larger ones such as Philadelphia, Baltimore, or Cincinnati had four or more. Jewish leaders regularly expressed impatience with all these divisions and pressed for unity. They argued that what Jews held in common was far more important than the liturgical differences that divided them, and they condemned the situation in cities like New York where five or more Jewish rites competed. But since similar divisions characterized any number of American religious groups—French Catholics and Irish Catholics worshiped apart, so did Lutherans of different backgrounds, and in one Cincinnati county there were four different Baptist churches reflecting four different points of origin—arguments for unity frequently fell on deaf ears. In some Jewish circles, in fact, the smorgasbord of worship choices even drew praise, perhaps a reflection of new marketplace values. "The Israelites living here come from various countries," one immigrant wrote back to his relatives in Bamberg approvingly. "Everybody can choose freely where or in which synagogue he wants to be enrolled."[17]

Actually many Jews chose not to enroll in any synagogue whatsoever. In America, unlike in Germany, the state placed no pressure on Jews to affiliate with a religious community, and in any case, thousands of Jews had settled in remote areas where no synagogues could be found. Discounting the smaller congregations that the census missed and the young children who would have been left at home, it seems reasonable to assume that as many as half of America's Jews were unaffiliated at midcentury. Jewish leaders took this to be a matter of grave concern.

Diversity, many at the time believed, posed a threat to the longtime viability of the American Jewish community. They looked to unify Jews through an overarching authority ("chief rabbi"), a conference of rabbis, or perhaps a unified prayer book, what Isaac Mayer Wise called "Minhag Amerika." Without unity and centralized authority, they warned, Judaism would decline. Like so many before and after them, they feared that America would prove to be a land that was good for Jews but bad for Judaism.

Paradoxically, though, diversity triumphed as mid-nineteenth-century Jews pursued three different strategies to try to ensure Judaism's survival. Some argued that Jews themselves needed to be "regenerated" through a greater emphasis on Jewish education and the strengthening of Jewish religious life. Others insisted that Judaism as a religion was at fault and needed to be "reformed." Still others felt that community and kinship, rather than rituals and faith, should form the new basis for Jewish life; they sought to unite Jews around ties of peoplehood.

The first strategy, perhaps best articulated by the great Orthodox Jewish leader Isaac Leeser, advocated tradition in an American key. Leeser called for greater emphasis on Jewish education, decorum, aesthetics, and an English-language sermon but nothing that deviated from Jewish law. Years after he himself had passed from the scene, those whom he influenced continued to pursue the goal of an Americanized traditional Judaism, insisting that Judaism's future depended upon the education and uplifting of American Jews rather than upon any fundamental changes to Judaism itself. A later generation would call this "modern orthodoxy."

The second strategy, made famous by Wise, the great Reform Jewish leader, presumed that Judaism itself needed to change in order for it to survive. Reformers urged Jews to abandon rituals that seemed incompatible with modernity and to adopt innovations that promised to make Judaism more appealing and spiritually uplifting, like shorter services, vernacular prayers, organ music, and mixed seating. "We hold that all such Mosaic and rabbinical laws as regulate diet, priestly purity, and dress originated in ages and under the influence of ideas entirely foreign to our present mental and spiritual state," the famed 1885 Pittsburgh Platform of Reform Judaism declared. "Their observance in our days," it continued, "is apt rather to obstruct than to further modern spiritual elevation." Reformers advocated thoroughgoing reforms—the removal of what they saw as Judaism's accumulated "defects and deformities"—to keep Judaism alive and lure young Jews back to the synagogue.[18]

The third strategy aimed at preserving Judaism in America rejected the synagogue altogether and focused on ties of peoplehood as the unifying element in Jewish life. This idea found its most important institutional expression in the Jewish fraternal organization B'nai B'rith (literally, "sons of the covenant"), established in 1843. The preamble to the order's original constitution carefully avoided any mention of God, Torah, ritual commandments, or religious faith but stressed the importance of Jewish unity: "B'nai B[']rith has taken upon itself the mission of uniting Israelites in the work of promoting their highest interests and those of humanity." While synagogues divided Jews and alienated some of them altogether, B'nai B'rith argued that fraternal ties—the covenant (b'rith) that bound Jews one to another regardless of religious ideology—could bring about "union and harmony."[19]

The three strategies put forth to save American Judaism, in addition to being three means of achieving a common preservationist end, also reflected deep uncertainty surrounding the central priorities of American Jewish religious life. Which of their core values, Jews wondered, should be priority number one: (1) to uphold and maintain Judaism's sacred religious traditions, (2) to adapt Judaism to new conditions of life in a new land, or (3) to preserve above all a strong sense of Jewish peoplehood and communal unity? Many Jews, traditionalists and reformers alike, actually cherished all three of these values. The history of American Judaism is replete with oscillations back and forth among these priorities, a reflection of tensions, deeply rooted within Judaism itself, between the forces of tradition and the forces of change, between those who supported compromise for the sake of unity and those who insisted upon firmness for the sake of principle.

Looking back these tensions may be seen to have been highly beneficial. Proponents of different strategies and priorities in American Jewish life checked each other's excesses. Together they accomplished what none might have accomplished separately: they kept American Judaism going. But it is important to recognize, at the same time, that this benefit came at a steep price. Often, and even to this very day, American Jewish religious life, because of its great diversity, has seethed with acrimonious contention, the unseemly specter of Jews battling Jews. The question, not so different from the one facing Jews in the mid-nineteenth century, remains where to compromise for the sake of unity and where to stand firm for the sake of principle.

With so many questions and issues and tensions confronting them, it comes as no surprise that as they approach their 350th anniversary on American soil, Jews feel bewildered and uncertain. Should they embrace intermarriage as an opportunity for outreach or condemn it as a disaster for their offspring? Build religious bridges or fortify religious boundaries? Strengthen religious authority or promote religious autonomy? Harmonize Judaism with contemporary culture or uphold Jewish tradition against contemporary culture? Compromise for the sake of Jewish unity or stand firm for cherished Jewish principles? Simultaneously, indeed, Jews witness two contradictory trends operating in their community: assimilation and revitalization. Which will predominate and what the future holds nobody knows. That will be determined day by day, community by community, Jew by Jew.

Regularly American Jews hear, as I did at the start of my career from the rabbinical-school scholar and as other Jews did in colonial times in the era of the American Revolution, in the nineteenth century, and in the twentieth century, that Judaism in America is doomed, that assimilation and intermarriage are inevitable. Should high rates of intermarriage continue and should the community grow complacent, that may yet prove true.

But history, as we have seen, also suggests another possibility: that today, as so often before, American Jews will find creative ways to maintain and revitalize American Judaism. With the help of visionary leaders, committed followers, and generous philanthropists, it may still be possible for the current "vanishing" generation of American Jews to be succeeded by another "vanishing" generation, and then still another.

Notes

1. *National Advocate,* December 5, 1825, 2.

2. Joseph L. Blau and Salo W. Baron, *The Jews of the United States: A Documentary History, 1790–1840* (New York: Columbia University Press, 1963), 2:542–45; *Christian Inquirer,* September 17, 1825, 151.

3. David de Sola Pool, *An Old Faith in the New World: Portrait of Shearith Israel, 1654–1954* (New York: Columbia University Press, 1955), 437.

4. Israel Goldstein, *A Century of Judaism in New York: B'nai Jeshurun, 1825–1925* (New York: Congregation B'nai Jeshurun, 1930), 54–55. The original spelling of the congregation's name is B'nai Yeshiorun.

5. Robert Liberles, "Conflict over Reforms: The Case of Congregation Beth Elohim, Charleston, South Carolina," in *The American Synagogue: A Sanctuary Transformed,* ed. Jack Wertheimer (Cambridge, U.K.: Cambridge University Press, 1987), 282.

6. Gary Phillip Zola, *Isaac Harby of Charleston, 1788–1828* (Tuscaloosa: University of Alabama Press, 1994), 112–49.

7. Jonathan D. Sarna, *A Great Awakening: The Transformation that Shaped Twentieth-Century American Judaism and Its Implications for Today* (New York: CIJE, 1995), 7.

8. Oliver A. Rink, "Private Interest and Godly Gain: The West India Company and the Dutch Reformed Church in New Netherland, 1624–1664," *New York History* 75 (1994): 245–64.

9. Samuel Oppenheim, "The Early History of the Jews in New York, 1654–1664," *Publications of the American Jewish Historical Society* 18 (1909): 4, 5, 20.

10. Ibid., 8–37.

11. E. T. Corwin, ed., *Ecclesiastical Records of the State of New York* (Albany: University of the State of New York, 1901), 1:530.

12. Jonathan D. Sarna and David G. Dalin, *Religion and State in the American Jewish Experience* (Notre Dame, Ind.: University of Notre Dame Press, 1997), 63–75; Philip B. Kurland and Ralph Lerner, *The Founders' Constitution* (Indianapolis, Ind.: Liberty Fund, 1987), iv, 638.

13. Blau and Baron, *Jews of the United States,* 8–11; Sarna and Dalin, *Religion and State,* 79–82.

14. Ira Rosenwaike, "An Estimate and Analysis of the Jewish Population of the United States in 1790," *Publications of the American Jewish Historical Society* 59 (1960): 23–67.

15. Jacob R. Marcus, *United States Jewry, 1776–1985,* 4 vols. (Detroit, Mich.: Wayne State University Press, 1989), 1:610–13.

16. Rudolf Glanz, "The Spread of Jewish Communities through America before the Civil War," *Yivo Annual* 15 (1974): 7–45; Rudolf Glanz, "Where the Jewish Press Was Distributed in Pre–Civil War America," *Western States Jewish Historical Quarterly* 5 (1972): 1–14; and Uriah Z. Engelman, "Jewish Statistics in the U.S. Census of Religious Bodies (1850–1935)," *Jewish Social Studies* 9 (1947): 130.

17. Abraham J. Karp, "Overview: The Synagogue in America—A Historical Typology," in American Synagogue, ed.Wertheimer, 5.

18. Pittsburgh Platform, in *Response to Modernity: A History of the Reform Movement in Judaism,* Michael A. Meyer (New York: Oxford University Press, 1988), 387–88.

19. Edward E. Grusd, *B'nai B'rith: The Story of a Covenant* (New York: Appleton-Century, 1966), 20.

Catholicism and American Freedom

John T. McGreevy

Catholicism and American Freedom (CAAF) sketches the interplay between Catholic and American ideas of freedom, beginning in the 1840s, when an unprecedented wave of European immigrants made Catholicism the single-largest religious denomination in the United States.[1] Many of these immigrants helped create what historians now describe as the nineteenth-century Catholic revival.[2] The revival affected large regions of France, Belgium, Germany, and Italy and swept across Ireland and into the United States, Canada, parts of Latin America, and Australia. Mass attendance became more regular, and religious vocations (especially among young women) grew steadily. *Ultramontanism,* the term most associated with the revival, is shorthand for a cluster of shifts that included a Vatican-fostered move to Thomistic philosophy, a more intense experiential piety centered on miracles and Vatican-approved devotions such as the Sacred Heart, an international outlook suspicious of national variations within Catholicism, and a heightened respect for church authorities ranging from the pope to parish priests. All this was nurtured in the world of Catholic parishes, schools, and associations, whose members often understood themselves as arrayed against the wider society.[3]

What this revival and its intellectual legacy meant for the history of the United States is my subject. The story moves from nineteenth-century debates over education, slavery, and nationalism to twentieth- and twenty-first-century discussions of social-welfare policy, democracy, birth control, abortion, and sexual abuse. Questions asked include: Why did so few Catholics urge the abolition of slavery, and why were so many abolitionists anti-Catholic? Why did anti-Catholicism so powerfully shape American political and intellectual life in the late nineteenth century (as it did in much

From *Historically Speaking* 6 (September/October 2004)

of Europe and Latin America)? How did Catholic ideas of the economy coalesce with those of the Democratic Party in the 1930s? How did Catholic ideas about human sexuality and human life split apart from leaders in that party in the 1960s? And finally how can historians of the United States place what is arguably the central religious event of the twentieth century, the Second Vatican Council (1962–65), into the narrative of American history?

A guiding assumption is that the interplay between Catholic and American remains poorly understood. In part this is because many influential modern Catholic thinkers—Jaime Balmes from Spain, Joseph Kleutgen, Heinrich Pesch, Karl Rahner, and Bernard Haring from Germany, Matteo Liberatore from Italy, John Henry Newman from England, Charles Montalembert, Jacques Maritain, Yves Congar, Marie-Dominique Chenu, and Henri de Lubac from France, Bernard Lonergan from Canada, Gustavo Gutierrez from Peru, and Karol Wojtyla (John Paul II) from Poland—did not always (or ever) write in English or work in the United States.

At the same time historians of the United States seem to have agreed with an 1861 *New York Times* editorial announcing that "intelligent minds in every country" thought Catholic belief a "fast-vanishing quality."[4] In contrast to colleagues studying Europe and Latin America, historians of the United States have evinced little interest in the ideas sustaining Catholic institutions (thousands of churches, the world's largest private school system, the nation's largest social-welfare agencies, the world's largest chain of private hospitals) and communicants. Most historians of the United States know less about American Catholic intellectual life, even less about important figures such as Orestes Brownson and John Courtney Murray, than a "republican" tradition already in decline by the late eighteenth century or a socialism distinguished in the United States by its brevity.

Measuring the Catholic contribution to American intellectual life also entails assessing the role played by Catholicism (and anti-Catholicism) in the American intellectual imagination. The topic is not sufficiently studied, in part because anti-Catholicism directed against Catholic individuals declined sharply after the 1920s, even as more subtle prejudices against hierarchy and authority continued to shape American intellectual life.

My hope is to capture two traditions in motion, not one: to explore American ideas about Catholicism along with the predispositions (at times blinders) framing the mental landscape of American Catholics.

Notes

1. On May 7, 2004, the Historical Society and the Intercollegiate Studies Institute cohosted a forum on McGreevy's book at ISI's headquarters in Wilmington,

Delaware. McGreevy opened with a brief synopsis of his *Catholicism and American Freedom* (2003), after which Leo Ribuffo and Christopher Shannon provided commentary, and then McGreevy responded. Edited versions of the participants' comments appear here.

2. Raymond Grew terms the conflict between Catholicism and liberalism a "central theme" of nineteenth-century European history. See Grew, "Liberty and the Catholic Church in 19th-Century Europe," in *Freedom and Religion in the 19th Century,* ed. Richard Helmstadter (Stanford, Calif.: Stanford University Press, 1997), 197; Margaret Lavinia Anderson, "The Limits of Secularization: On the Problem of the Catholic Revival in 19th-Century Germany," *Historical Journal* 38 (1995): 647–70; and Austin Iverveigh, ed., *The Politics of Religion in an Age of Revival: Studies in 19th-Century Europe and Latin America* (London: Institute of Latin American Studies, 2000).

3. Joseph A. Komonchak, "Modernity and the Construction of Roman Catholicism," *Cristianesimo nella storia* 18 (1997): 353–85.

4. "The French Press and the Roman Church," *New York Times,* February 2, 1861, 4.

The American Catholic Church and Ordered Liberty

Leo P. Ribuffo

For more than two centuries harsh nativists, relatively benign critics, and reflexive Protestant celebrationists have called the Roman Catholic Church an un-American institution. While dispensing with the loaded term *un-American,* we need to take the issue seriously. In several respects, some obvious and some harder to discern, the Catholic Church *as an institution* has stood apart from *prevailing* American attitudes.

First, and most obviously, as George Marsden has observed in *The Soul of the American University* (1994), the United States is the "only modern nation" whose "dominant culture was substantially shaped by low-church Protestantism." Some Scots, Swiss, and Canadians might dispute the "only," but Marsden's general point is sound. Second, and less obviously at a time when scholars exaggerate American diversity past and present, the United States was conceived by leaders with an extraordinary sense of *national* mission. This sense of mission, which derived both from Reformation Protestantism and from Enlightenment republicanism, sometimes involved changing the rest of the world by example and sometimes involved changing the rest of the world by force of arms. Indeed, despite notable internal divisions, this sense of mission energized Americans to conquer a continent within a half century of independence, a conquest that in turn further energized nationalist sentiment. In this patriotic, even chauvinist climate, the Catholic Church was—and still is—an *international* organization headed by a foreigner. Not surprisingly the Vatican classified the United States as a mission field until 1908, well after it had become the foremost economy on Earth.

From *Historically Speaking* 6 (September/October 2004)

Third, since roughly the 1840s, the United States has been a democracy. Political democracy, though limited almost entirely to white men at the outset, nonetheless went far beyond what was available in Europe. An expandable ethos of equality was at least as important, and the results quickly could be seen within Protestantism. In the eighteenth century Jonathan Edwards would have agreed with all of the popes that the true faith could not be defined by every Tom, Dick, or Hezekiah who happened to read scripture. In the nineteenth century Barton Stone, Charles Grandison Finney, and Joseph Smith had no such qualms. The Catholic Church was not—and is not—a democracy. Indeed, as McGreevy stresses, while Americans on the whole became increasingly democratic and enthusiastic about individual autonomy, the Vatican and elements of the American Church became less so.

Throughout much of his book, perhaps most of it, McGreevy in theory seems to prefer this more restrained definition of freedom, which might be called, with a bow to traditionalist conservatives, ordered liberty. What he likes about it, however, would not please staunch libertarians. From Orestes Brownson through "Right Reverend New Dealer" John Ryan to the contemporary bishops, Catholic clerics and thinkers in McGreevy's book question laissez-faire, endorse federal economic regulation, and support the welfare state.

At the same time, writing in neutral prose and making due allowance for internal divisions and debate, McGreevy shows that the Church frequently opposed the expansion of personal freedom as most Americans understood the concept. This was true long before the contemporary controversy over abortion. Indeed the Church not only gave de facto support to slavery and helped to enforce censorship but also backed restrictions on birth control for non-Catholics. These positions were not uniquely Catholic, but the Church's power should not be understated.

Part of the explanation is that final authority in the Catholic Church is held by a foreigner. In the nineteenth century James Cardinal Gibbons tried to comfort Protestant America with the notion that the doctrine of papal infallibility was no more mysterious than the Supreme Court serving as the final interpreter of the Constitution. Perhaps so, but the Catholic Supreme Court, so to speak, resides in Rome rather than Washington and thus is less responsive to American opinions. Probably papal misunderstanding of the United States has been no worse than that of most European heads of government. This is not a very high standard, however. On the contrary, the papacy has often seemed to reflect European clichés about American hyperpower, mindless materialism, and a confusion of freedom with license.

Certainly the Vatican seems more likely to censure a characteristic American religious syncretism—of Catholicism and democracy—than Third World religious adaptations in which Catholicism merges with voodoo or animism.

But to what extent have the clergy and leading theologians represented the American Catholicism in McGreevy's title? I wish that McGreevy had called his book *The Catholic Church and Ordered Liberty.* Lay Catholics do not appear often enough in this book. Even Al Smith, Joseph McCarthy, and John Kennedy, symbols of Catholicism to most of the country, are treated too briefly. And where is Phyllis Schlafly, probably the most influential Catholic woman in U.S. history? Perhaps McGreevy's perspective merely reflects the fact of Catholic hierarchy. It is hard to imagine a book on the relationship between freedom and Baptists, Methodists, or even Presbyterians that paid so little attention to the laity. But, even if he had wanted to, Al Smith could not have played so prominent a role in the Catholic Church of the 1920s as William Jennings Bryan did among Presbyterians, who were both less hierarchical and less controlled by the clergy.

What has it meant to be an American Catholic? Do we routinely include in this category most immigrants from predominantly Catholic countries, no matter how indifferent to religion? Does this label require church attendance, and if so, must attendance occur more than twice a year? What about so-called cultural Catholics, who no longer practice that religion or perhaps any other but who still nonetheless bear some markings from the faith of their childhood?

Although scholars are attentive to this conceptual issue, it has rarely bothered harsh nativists, relatively benign critics, or reflexive Protestant celebrationists. They have not only exaggerated the cohesion of the Church as an institution but they have also been remarkably obtuse about the behavior of ordinary Catholics. Paying too much attention to words and not enough to deeds, they somehow found among disorderly Irish and Italian immigrants a docile population subservient to priests and nuns. Too often even scholars read back into earlier eras the so-called traditional values that characterized Catholicism in the 1950s (or, more precisely, the stereotypical, placid 1950s). For good and ill American Catholics went their own ways long before they ignored papal bans on birth control. For example while the Vatican worried about United States hyperpower 150 years before the term was coined, this power certainly appealed to the Catholics who served disproportionately in the American military since the War of 1812. As McGreevy reminds us, conservative Catholic theologians condemned strategic bombing during World War II (to their credit, in my opinion). I doubt that this disapproval was widely shared by the Catholics who probably were the largest religious denomination in the Marine Corps. While many Civil War–era Catholics applauded their bishops' opposition to the Union's war against slavery, Catholics in the 1970s showed no such enthusiasm for bishops who favored busing to redress the legacy of slavery and segregation.

Although harsh nativists, relatively benign critics, and reflexive Protestant celebrationists have often misunderstood American Catholics, they have raised interesting questions amid their heated rhetoric. One of the most interesting is the relationship between, on the one hand, Protestantism and Catholicism—and we might add Islam—and, on the other, the development of capitalism, economic prosperity, and political democracy. I don't know what Max Weber would say, but many of the freest and most prosperous countries in the world have predominantly Protestant populations with large Catholic minorities—not only the United States but also Canada, Germany, Australia, and the Netherlands. Moving from grand theory to anecdote, there is some truth to nativist Josiah Strong's belief that when Catholics rebel, they really rebel. Catholicism's gifts to the American Left include Populist Mary Lease, Communist Elizabeth Gurley Flynn, and New Leftist Tom Hayden.

Two important questions are implicit on every page of McGreevy's book. First, what is the difference between bigotry and legitimate conflict about religion or public issues related to religion? For the leading social thinkers of the 1950s—pluralist social scientists and consensus historians like Daniel Bell, Seymour Martin Lipset, and Richard Hofstadter—there was essentially no difference. Questions about ethics, these thinkers argued, should be kept out of the public sphere because they threaten the necessary but fragile social consensus; anybody who raises them is probably an "extremist" burdened with status anxiety and a paranoid style. Although the vocabulary has changed, many contemporary multiculturalists share an analogous vision of a society without cultural conflict. And even pundits and politicians devoid of serious ideas believe that no one should say, "My religion is better than your religion."

Although admirable in many ways, this tolerant vision has several defects, not the least of which is that it fails to intersect with reality. Even during the relatively placid 1950s, as John Courtney Murray emphasized at the time, Protestant-Catholic conflict was endemic beneath a thin veneer of politeness. One of McGreevy's foremost accomplishments is to rediscover that conflict and explore its nuances. In the post-1960s world in which both individual self-expression and cultural diversity are increasingly cherished, conflicts related to religion are more open and visible—and not just between Catholics and Protestants or secularists. Is Mel Gibson's conservative Catholic portrayal of the crucifixion anti-Semitic (mildly so, in my view)? Does anti-Zionism differ from anti-Semitism (yes in theory but the line is often crossed)? Is a Muslim now considered as American as Will Herberg's prototypical "Protestant-Catholic-Jew" (yes in theory but usually not in fact)? Such questions are painful and not always easy to answer. Yet they need to be addressed with civility in Murray's special sense of the term—as serious questions worthy of serious argument. This means (as Hofstadter, Bell, and Lipset might warn) that such questions probably should not be asked of or answered by presidential candidates.

The second important issue implicit on every page of McGreevy's book is the extent to which Catholics have differed from most other Americans. As I have already suggested, McGreevy seems to overstate the differences, at least for the period before Vatican II and the 1960s. This is partly because he pays excessive attention to words. On the one hand the Protestant-dominated culture was never as individualist as the prevailing rhetoric implied. Even John Dewey favored the construction of a "common faith" and thought the right educational system could help to construct it. Americans gathered often in their lodges, VFW halls, or Ku Klux Klan chapters. On the other hand Catholic denunciations of "excessive selfishness" (the bishops in 1919) or "perverse individualism" (Father Ryan in *A Living Wage*) need to be examined more critically. Too often their calls for "solidarity" lacked real intellectual content, let alone effective policy prescriptions. Anyone to the left of Ayn Rand could join in a repudiation of "*excessive* selfishness" or "*perverse* individualism."

The differences between native-born Catholics and Protestants have certainly diminished during the past half-century. To recall comedian Lenny Bruce's phrase, Catholics are now less likely to claim that their church is the "only *the* Church." However good this trend is for Catholics as individuals or for American society in general, it is a mixed blessing for the Church as an institution. After all if nostalgia rather than supernatural belief binds cosmopolitan Catholics to a church with which they disagree on major issues, why not just walk down the street to join the high mass led by an Episcopal priest who accepts gay rights, birth control, and abortion?

Comments on Catholicism and American Freedom

Christopher Shannon

John McGreevy is the Jay Dolan of his generation. I mean this not only in the sense of his being the leading practitioner of American Catholic history today but also in his default capacity as ambassador from this subfield to the larger profession. Dolan burst onto the professional scene with his 1975 monograph *The Immigrant Church.* Scholars not particularly interested in church history were drawn to the work as a study of immigrants, and Dolan's use of then cutting-edge techniques of social history placed his book at the vanguard of the academic history of its day. Twenty or so years later McGreevy burst on to the scene with his *Parish Boundaries* (1996). Here the innovation was less in method than subject matter: the book examined the role of urban Catholics in the resistance to integrated housing during the civil rights era. Race, an issue relatively neglected by Dolan, had become the single most burning passion of American historians following the end of the Cold War. Non-Catholic historians praised *Parish Boundaries* for its sensitivity to religion as a "factor" in race relations; Catholic historians praised it for being praised by non-Catholics. *Parish Boundaries* appealed to those within the field as a model of yet another "new" American Catholic history that would finally realize the long dreamed of integration into the mainstream of the profession—precisely the hope for Dolan's *Immigrant Church* some twenty years earlier.

I raise these connections less out of concern for professional genealogies than as a symptom of a logic of revision that afflicts the profession as a whole. For reasons that I believe are in the book itself, I doubt that *Catholicism and*

From *Historically Speaking* 6 (September/October 2004)

American Freedom will succeed where Dolan's work failed. It does stand, however, as a ringing endorsement of the professional standards to which post-Dolan American Catholic historians still aspire. It is appropriate to evaluate the book at a level that can unfortunately best be identified as metahistory.

Circumstances, alas, leave me little alternative. In purely professional terms the book is a nearly flawless monograph. Any minor imperfections worth mentioning have been nigglingly hashed out in the numerous reviews and symposiums that have greeted the book in the scant year since its publication. In the context of McGreevy's career, moreover, the book arrives not simply as his latest contribution to scholarship but also as an implicit statement about the nature of historical scholarship in general. The years since *Parish Boundaries* saw McGreevy somewhat reluctantly drawn into the debate on "Christian scholarship," a particular manifestation of the broader postmodern challenge to modernist professional history writing, a challenge that in large part accounts for the existence of the Historical Society. In religious history circles McGreevy has been the leading defender of the liberal modernist center against the modest perspectivalism advanced by George Marsden. Hardly postmodernist in the strong Nietzschean sense, Marsden has simply argued that a distinctly Christian approach to history deserves a seat at the table with Marxist, feminist, and other perspectives; offering Christian scholarship as a kind of Galbraithean countervailing power to balance the secular bias in mainstream history writing, Marsden in no way questions the pseudoscientific-research techniques that provide the profession with its intellectual legitimacy. This modest proposal, however, has proved too extreme for McGreevy, who takes his stand with Thomas Haskell in defending conventional historical practice circa 1986, right before the linguistic turn appeared on the radar screen of the *American Historical Review.*

At first glance a reading of *Catholicism and American Freedom* might suggest that even Haskell is too extreme for McGreevy's professional sensibilities. In his best-known defense of the profession Haskell has conceded that "objectivity is not neutrality," a formulation that ultimately boils down to the blunt—one might say rather Nietzschean—admission that "objective" professional history does serve power, albeit the power of a liberal social order dedicated to the advance of human freedom. I believe that McGreevy would be proud to say that he offers no such statement of political purpose in his book, but the lack of any such statement might leave those unfamiliar with American Catholic history wondering just why historians should be concerned with the tension between Catholicism and American freedom. McGreevy notes that American Catholics make up roughly 25 percent of the

U.S. population, yet have failed to receive the scholarly attention lavished on numerically less significant phenomena, such as a socialism McGreevy wryly notes has been "distinguished in the United States by its brevity." Of course, history, even quantitative history, has never been simply about numbers. Intellectuals, minorities, and now homosexuals merit a monograph quota all out of proportion to their numbers in the population; women have yet to receive their fair share. The choice of subject matter in history is a question of values, and professional historians have tended to focus on groups that embody—or, alternatively, directly threaten—the cherished values of good liberal professionals. McGreevy makes clear in his book that American Catholicism does not fit neatly into either side of the great morality play of liberal history; he refuses to acknowledge that hostility to this real cultural otherness on the part of liberal historians accounts for the relatively understudied status of American Catholic history.

As a statement of purpose McGreevy offers the neutral, scholarly rationale that the "interplay between Catholic and American remains poorly understood." To this I respond, poorly understood by whom? By Thomas Haskell and David Hollinger? Yes, for reasons I have just mentioned. By Jay Dolan, Phillip Gleason, David O'Brien, Patrick Carey, and the subsequent generation of American Catholic historians who have read their work? I think not. Dolan and his cohort understood all too well that Catholicism did not fit into conventional liberalism and in turn dedicated their professional lives to trying to make it fit. If Dolan wrote as an outsider trying to get into the mainstream, McGreevy writes as a relative insider secure enough to consider the world we have lost. This position served him well in his first book, *Parish Boundaries.* Acknowledging, and scolding, the racism of urban Catholics in the 1960s, McGreevy also expressed sympathy for the communal ethos of urban parishes—a cultural luxury not available to the upwardly mobile, middle-class professionals of Dolan's era, whose revolt against the parish served to mark their entry into that elusive "mainstream." Though clearly in debt to more popular, nonacademic accounts such as J. Anthony Lukacs's *Common Ground, Parish Boundaries* marked a real contribution to a scholarly literature too quick simply to dismiss urban Catholics as racists.

Catholicism and American Freedom employs a similar conceptual framework but ultimately to less effect. Again we have a sympathetic, balanced account of Catholic communalism, though now with particular respect to its understanding of the dangerously antinomian view of autonomy implicit in the liberal understanding of American freedom. In depth and scope the book certainly promises to be a great leap forward for American Catholic history.

McGreevy's focus on the concept of autonomy, as opposed to a more indigenous concept such as liberty, raises the philosophical stakes of the work; his ambitious chronological range, from the mid-nineteenth century to the present, suggests a new synthesis in the making. Strangely what we end up with is a work whose interpretation of the tension between Catholicism and American freedom is at its core fundamentally indistinguishable from the grand narrative offered by Dolan in his *American Catholic Experience* (1985), a work that has already received a major, and beautifully written, retelling in Charles Morris's *American Catholic* (1997) and again by Dolan himself in his recent *In Search of American Catholicism* (2002).

Conspicuously absent from McGreevy's work is Dolan's repeated invocation of early-nineteenth-century lay trusteeism as a model of a viable, democratic American Catholicism; still in McGreevy's concluding characterization of the "halting Catholic endorsement of slave emancipation, democracy and religious freedom" and of Catholicism's "belated recognition of the importance of individual human dignity," we have the familiar story of Catholicism as cultural lag. Only in the area of labor relations does Catholicism seem ahead of the curve, but even bitter, Vatican II–era liberals like Dolan conceded this point. My question to McGreevy is: What exactly are you trying to say that is different from what Jay Dolan has already said?

I would like to venture one answer to this question as a way of getting at some of the deeper historiographical problems suggested by this undeniably excellent work of professional history. McGreevy's new twist on Dolan's old story lies in his internationalization of American Catholic history. Gone is Dolan's quest to tell the story of the American Church in American terms; inspired by the work of James Kloppenberg and Daniel Rogers, McGreevy wishes to understand American Catholicism in terms of its transatlantic connections. Does he mean to say that the Roman Catholic Church, a self-identified universal Church well known by historians for its repeated attacks on nationalism, is best understood in international terms? Well, what could be more obvious? In fact it was quite obvious to the generation of American Catholic historians who preceded Dolan and against whom Dolan advanced his Americanist school of Catholic history. The line between revision and recycling blurs. In this, as in so many other things, American Catholic historians have simply followed their non-Catholic mentors. Intellectual histories of the Progressive and New Deal eras written during the 1950s and early 1960s routinely made note of the European models that inspired American reformers; by the late 1960s the search for an indigenous American radicalism, particularly as pursued through the narrowly empirical methods of the new social history, rendered these European connections passé. The profession revived the international story in the 1990s, partly in its ongoing effort to appear newly improved but also as a desperate attempt to keep liberal and social democratic hopes alive after a decade of Reaganism and the fall of the Berlin wall.

That the story of American Catholicism could be something other than the story of American liberalism is suggested by McGreevy's chapters on "Life," a euphemism for birth control and abortion. These are by far the freshest chapters in the book, largely because they deal with a subject that has yet to receive adequate treatment in the historiography of American Catholicism. Here McGreevy's otherwise frustrating balance comes as something of a relief, if only because most of the non-Catholic histories of the subject have been written from a stridently prochoice perspective. In these chapters we have glimpses of a truly radical moment in American history. As McGreevy writes, "In 1973 pro-choice activists could still term Senator Edward Kennedy's position on abortion 'thoroughly revolting.' Two years later . . . Kennedy led the fight against any effort to restrict federal funding of abortions through the Medicaid program." How did this happen? My sentimental Democratic heart bleeds to read of prounion, prolife Democrats in Michigan who in the years before *Roe v. Wade* opposed liberalization of the state's abortion laws even as they worked to extend welfare benefits to poor women trying to raise the children that prochoice activists were trying to consign to the category of "unwanted." By 1980 a prolife Democrat would become more rare than a black Republican. It would take a book at least as long as *Catholicism and American Freedom* to describe, if not explain, these changes. I suppose this is the book I wish McGreevy had written.

On the eve of the Civil War, abolitionists equated Catholicism with slavery and declared Catholics unfit for democratic citizenship. Catholics in turn charged that the ideal of unfettered individual freedom upheld by abolitionists would lead to moral and social anarchy. How you assess these propositions will determine how you track the history of Catholicism and American freedom; this assessment in turn depends on how you judge the issue of abortion. McGreevy offers no such judgment. Cardinal Joseph Bernardin emerges as a kind of moral compass, though in his capacity as a public figure he tended to emphasize the more liberal-friendly dimensions of the Church's "consistent life ethic," such as care for the poor and opposition to nuclear war. John Noonan clearly shines as a model American Catholic intellectual, which suggests a "birth control yes, abortion no" assessment of the limits to Catholic liberalism.

Still against what I take to be McGreevy's best intentions, the most heroic figure of all may just be grumpy, old, intransigent John Ford (the moral theologian, not the film director). Denouncing birth control and saturation bombing in the 1940s, decades before the phrase "consistent life ethic" came into common usage among Catholics, Ford saw in modern attitudes toward sex a slippery slope toward abortion, eugenics, and euthanasia. History has borne out his fears, yet historians have yet to bestow on him the mantle of prophet. On "life" issues he had a foresight comparable to W. E. B. Du Bois' pronouncements on the future of the color line in America. Yet the history presented in *Catholicism and American Freedom* cannot bring itself to see "life" as an issue of equivalent moral gravity. The power of McGreevy's earlier work, *Parish Boundaries,* derives from its dramatic presentation of the tragic confrontation between two goods: the struggle for racial justice and the integrity of local communities. For most of *Catholicism and American Freedom,* tragic conflict gives way to an evasive "tension." By the end of the discussion of "life," even this comparatively tame tension dissipates for lack of sufficient moral focus. The book ends with a whimper rather than a bang. This may indeed reflect the actual state of American Catholicism today. However even Thomas Haskell would concede that objective history involves the imposition of some inescapably moral interpretive framework on the flux of reality. McGreevy's straining after neutrality on "life" issues appears less a heroic achievement of objectivity than an abdication of interpretive responsibility.

Response to Ribuffo and Shannon

John T. McGreevy

Leo Ribuffo challenges me to more fully integrate Catholic politicians and political activists into my account. Fair enough. In part my explanation for the modest attention devoted to John Kennedy, Al Smith, and Joseph McCarthy is that I wrote an intellectual history not a political one, and I do discuss how Catholic and non-Catholic intellectuals understood the Smith campaign in 1928 and Kennedy's handling of the religious issue in 1960. What does seem notable by its absence in CAAF, in retrospect, is a thorough treatment of religion and politics at the local level, where the parallels between the neighborhood-based, male-dominated parish structure and the neighborhood-based, male-dominated ward structure deserve much-closer attention.

Ribuffo adds that more sustained treatment of figures such as Phyllis Schlafly (or, I might add, William F. Buckley) would have widened the scope of a narrative too concerned with Catholic responses to American liberals at the expense of Catholic influence on the modern conservative movement. Again a reasonable point. Still fine books on the relationship between Catholics and modern conservatives do exist.[1] And within the one hundred thousand words bequeathed me by W. W. Norton, I thought it more important to focus on the dominant Catholic intellectual tradition—suspicious of liberalism, certainly, but dismissive (at least until the 1980s) of *National Review*–style, free-market economics.

Ribuffo also makes a broader claim: that I place too great an emphasis on "words" or more particularly "clergy and leading theologians" at the expense of studying the behavior of lay Catholics. Certainly I do not intend to argue that all lay Catholics reflexively obeyed priests and bishops. (And some of the

From *Historically Speaking* 6 (September/October 2004)

figures discussed at length in the book, including Orestes Brownson, James McMaster, and Jacques Maritain, were not priests.) Or that in "Catholic" immigrants to the United States from Italy, Germany, Ireland, Mexico, or anywhere else were Catholic in a meaningful sense. What I can do is point to a subculture of remarkable density and scope and ask what ideas and practices sustained it. That all Catholics did not agree upon or even care about the contours of those ideas and practices is unremarkable, and we should avoid placing upon Catholics a burden of coherence not impressed upon, say, followers of John Dewey.

Better simply to demonstrate that this subculture and its ideas had consequences. Three examples: 180,000 nuns worked in the United States by the 1960s, staffing the world's largest private school system and running the world's largest system of private hospitals. And yet we have many more competent books on Jane Addams and her circle at Hull House than on any aspect of the history of women religious. Or again: in the last two weeks I received two books for review, one a biography of Peace Corps leader and vice presidential candidate Sargent Shriver and one of 1968 presidential candidate Eugene McCarthy.[2] Both books emphasize the importance these men placed on Catholic social thought. McCarthy, in particular, was influenced by the work of French philosopher Jacques Maritain. But how many historians can spell Maritain? Or finally: I discuss at some length in CAAF the work of John Ford, S.J. (not, sigh, the movie director). Ford was perhaps the most influential American Catholic moral theologian in the two decades after World War II: advising bishops and cardinals on knotty ethical questions; publishing a two-volume history of his subject that was required reading in many seminaries; assisting a colleague in developing ethical guidelines on birth control, abortion, and euthanasia for Catholic hospitals; and writing a widely read yearly summary of the scholarly literature. (By the 1950s Ford's ideas about sin were probably influencing the practice of thousands of priests in hundreds of thousands of confessions.) In the mid-1960s Ford was the most prominent American involved in the successful effort to persuade Pope Paul VI to sustain the ban on "artificial" contraception.

Ribuffo notes that Ford's searing 1944 attack on American saturation-bombing campaigns in Germany had little effect. Quite true, but not because priests like Ford did not fairly "represent" a Catholicism dominated by patriotic laypeople. Bishops, not just Catholic lieutenants in the Marine Corps, evaded grappling with Ford's arguments precisely because they called into question the hard (and recently) won Catholic status as the most loyal of Americans. (But the story does not end there because Ford's essay became a touchstone in the literature on just war ethics and an inspiration to some 1960s Catholic peace activists.)[3] Ford's despair at the abandonment of Catholic teaching on birth control by virtually all Catholic couples by the 1970s *is* connected to his clerical status, but by then most priests disagreed with church teaching on birth control as well. These complications make me uneasy about Ribuffo's implied division between a popular religion of the people and a religion of "words" controlled by priests. Better to acknowledge and investigate tensions in what still seems to me a distinct intellectual and cultural tradition without anachronistically assuming that the primary dividing line is between leaders and led.

Christopher Shannon seems to find the narrative presented in CAAF convincing, and I am grateful for his enthusiasm. But Shannon regrets in harsh phrasing that I did not challenge the "pseudoscientific-research techniques that provide the profession with its intellectual legitimacy."

Goodness. Weary authors feel this most acutely, but Shannon rather casually glides by the effort required to get a compelling and persuasive story onto the page, a story that in this instance required a massive investment in archival research. It is striking that Shannon does not identify a single historical work meeting his exacting theological standards.

Of course my reference in the preceding paragraph to archival research may confirm for Shannon my imprisonment in the cage of "conventional historical practice." Following Thomas Haskell—and I hardly consider myself an important figure in this discussion—I have emphasized the importance of treating all historical actors with some measure of empathy. Haskell's own use of the term *ascetic* to describe the historian's stance as he or she tries to understand worldviews different from his/her own seems to me just right and an important marker distinguishing scholarship from (simply) politics in an intellectual world often cavalier about conflating the pair.[4]

To Shannon, if I read him right, this seems a mealy-mouthed "abdication of interpretive responsibility." Shouldn't, he seems to ask, a Catholic historian forthrightly identify his or her position on controversial issues, informing the reader where he or she stands on the death penalty, abortion, or income distribution?

I think not. I actually agree with Shannon that the secondary historical literature on abortion—with the exception of journalist Cynthia Gorney's brilliant account—treats antiabortion activists with less sympathy than historians customarily reserve for antebellum slaveholders. In David Garrow's wonderfully researched standard narrative, for example, Catholic opponents of the legalization of abortion are comic-book figures of reaction, standing athwart the social progress marked by *Roe v. Wade*.[5]

More puzzling is Shannon's suggestion that attempting to understand the viewpoints of all sides on this issue—how American liberals had long battled Catholic efforts to restrict access to contraception, which shaped the abortion debate; how the Catholic opposition to contraception and its unpopularity undermined Catholic teaching on abortion; how the fight for legal abortion could become for many women (Catholic and non-Catholic) intertwined with emancipation from patriarchal religious structures—is "straining after neutrality." Historians, after all, cannot resolve the abortion debate. But historical scholarship can sharpen our understanding of it, hardly a partisan or religious goal.

What worries me is a theological framework based on the premise that American freedom rests solely on contemporary capitalism. A prophetic stance against that view does tap into an important strand of contemporary Catholic intellectual life, whose most articulate exponents think Catholics of the 1960s, during the heady days of the Second Vatican Council, were far too sanguine about the character of modern Western culture. But prophetic stances breed their own complacencies, notably a condemnation of historical actors for accepting liberal capitalism, without providing (or even suggesting) a more ethical economic and social alternative.

A long (and often glorious) history, stretching from the first modern human-rights campaign for the abolition of slavery to contemporary demands for gay and lesbian rights, predisposes historians of the United States to frame their narratives around rights obtained and independence achieved. Such narratives exalt "identity" at the expense of social class, court rulings instead of economic structures, individuals as opposed to families. Autonomy—often the preferred term is *agency*—becomes a supreme moral good, never a situation of last resort. Emphasizing the embeddedness of the human person and the ways in which all of us remain dependent would not only be more consistent with Catholic social thought but might produce better (or at least more intriguing) histories as well.[6]

Notes

1. Patrick Allitt, *Catholic Intellectuals and Conservative Politics in America, 1950–1985* (Ithaca, N.Y.: Cornell University Press, 1993). Also see Rick Perlstein, *Before the Storm: Barry Goldwater and the Unmaking of the American Consensus* (New York: Hill and Wang, 2001).

2. Dominic Sandbrook, *Eugene McCarthy: The Rise and Fall of Postwar American Liberalism* (New York: Knopf, 2004); Scott Stossel, *Sarge: The Life and Times of Sargent Shriver* (Washington, D.C.: Smithsonian Books, 2004).

3. John C. Ford, "The Morality of Obliteration Bombing," *Theological Studies* 5 (1944): 261–309; Michael Walzer, *Just and Unjust Wars: A Moral Argument with Historical Illustrations* (New York: Basic Books, 1977), 34.

4. Thomas Haskell, *Objectivity Is Not Neutrality: Explanatory Schemes in History* (Baltimore, Md.: Johns Hopkins University Press, 1998), 145–73; John T. McGreevy, "Faith Histories," in *Religion, Scholarship, and Higher Education: Perspectives, Models, and Future Prospects,* ed. Andrea Sterk (Notre Dame, Ind.: University of Notre Dame Press, 2002), 63–75.

5. Cynthia Gorney, *Articles of Faith: A Frontline History of the Abortion Wars* (New York: Simon and Schuster, 1994); David Garrow, *Liberty and Sexuality: The Right to Privacy and the Making of Roe v. Wade* (New York: Scribner's, 1994).

6. For some of the same concerns from a different angle, see Walter Johnson, "On Agency," *Journal of Social History* 37 (2003): 113–24.

PART 3

Evangelicalism, Past and Present

The Great Awakening and the Contested Origins of American Evangelical Christianity

Thomas S. Kidd

From 1740 to 1743 a series of religious revivals known as the Great Awakening swept through America's British colonies, energizing the personal faith of thousands but also jeopardizing the traditional religious order. By 1743 the fervor of the Great Awakening had begun to cool, and evangelical leaders sought to memorialize the season of spiritual excitement by publishing accounts of the revivals. Signs of strain within the new evangelical movement appeared in those accounts. Many writers assured readers that the awakenings in their churches had remained sober and controlled. From New Jersey Jonathan Dickinson wrote to the evangelical magazine *The Christian History* that his church had seen very little of the "irregular heats" that had plagued other congregations. Only in two or three instances had disorderly "enthusiasm" broken out, and those cases were "easily and speedily regulated." Jonathan Parsons wrote from West Lyme Parish, Connecticut, that the joys displayed in the revival meetings were not "wild, enthusiastick Whims." An assembly of mostly evangelical ministers meeting in Boston in 1743 agreed that while the revivals on the whole had been godly, Satan had injected some "Irregularities and Extravagancies" into them. They warned other evangelicals against following "secret Impulses" as revelations from God, setting up untutored laymen as preachers, or opening illegal Separate congregations.[1]

Historians have typically understood the contest generated by the Great Awakening as a feud between "Old Lights" and "New Lights," but that dichotomy cannot account for the tensions expressed in these revival narratives. To be sure there was a debate between Old Lights and evangelical New Lights about whether the revivals were legitimate at all. This discussion was capped

From *Historically Speaking* 9 (September/October 2007)

by the verbose clash between Boston's Charles Chauncy and Northampton's Jonathan Edwards, whose positions are often regarded as defining the Awakening's competing sides. But the Old Light versus New Light dispute actually has limited explanatory value and obscures the most interesting struggle over the origins of evangelicalism. That contest proceeded between different kinds of evangelicals, the moderates and the radicals. Old Lights like Chauncy could denounce the awakenings as entirely bogus, but his protests were futile. The evangelical movement in America had been born, and once born rhetorical protests could not stop it. The more compelling question was: What kind of movement would evangelical Christianity become? Although moderates held the preponderance of power, radicals kept working to make the movement more mystical, populist, and democratic. While it often did not fulfill its potential, the radical impulse within evangelicalism supplied pre-Revolutionary America with one of its strongest resources of egalitarian thought.

Instead of Old Lights and New Lights, I propose that we should understand responses to the Great Awakening as three points on a continuum. In the middle were the moderate evangelicals, who originally supported the revivals but became concerned about the chaos they appeared to breed. On one end were the antirevivalists, or Old Lights, who dismissed the awakenings as overheated, disorderly emotion. At the continuum's other end were the radical evangelicals, who saw the revivals as the inauguration of a great era of power and revelation from the Holy Spirit. These positions were fluid and tenuous, and most key participants' and observers' stances moved along the continuum over time. In general devout people responded warmly to the beginning of the revivals, which was signaled by the appearance of the great English itinerant George Whitefield. Over time, though, many, like the assembled Boston ministers in 1743, began to doubt whether all the exotic phenomena associated with the revivals were of God. Figures like Edwards, New Jersey's Gilbert Tennent, and even the arch-radical James Davenport of Southold, Long Island, all moderated their initial zeal to some extent.

Radical participants in the Awakening, including many laypeople, not only expressed their piety in emotionally vivid ways but their excited behavior also seemed to threaten the social order. Their extremes caused many early sympathizers to express more reservations over time. Moderates winced as radicals questioned the traditional educational requirements for ministers and sought to ordain men of all races based on the blessing of the Spirit on their preaching. The zealots gave women, African Americans, and Native Americans more prominent roles than ever before in their churches. In some radical Baptist congregations, women served as deaconesses and eldresses.

Radicals encouraged laypeople of all kinds (including children) to exhort or testify authoritatively about God's dealings in their lives. They took seriously the ecstatic experiences of the people, such as dreams, trances, and visions, and saw these episodes as divinely sent. These Spirit-filled folks took upon themselves the right to critique pastors, especially those who seemed less than enthusiastic about the new season of grace. Finally some radicals violated colonial laws by opening unauthorized congregations that were fully devoted to the ministry of revival. While these characteristics may seem modest, in the context of mid-eighteenth-century American society, radical evangelicalism represented the first popular, widespread, Anglo-American uprising against established authority. It launched a social and cultural American revolution.

One can understand why antirevivalists, as well as moderate evangelicals, sought to contain the most radical manifestations of the Great Awakening, when put in its proper context. The evangelical uprising represented a direct assault on the authority of many established ministers. Untutored laymen concluded that they had as good a right to preach as the educated clergy who graduated from Harvard, Yale, or one of the British universities. Inspired by Whitefield, some evangelicals even raised questions about whether established ministers had experienced the "new birth" of salvation in Christ. Young evangelical itinerants barged into parishes and church buildings uninvited, created spiritual uproars, and drew followers away from more reserved ministers, some of whom had served their congregations faithfully for decades.

Antirevivalists claimed that these radicals revealed the actual aims of all revivalists and that "Whitefieldism" would ultimately lead to nothing but frenzied chaos. The moderate evangelicals insisted that the revivals could proceed without outlandish hubbub. The moderates sincerely delighted in the prospect of many hundreds of people experiencing the new birth almost simultaneously, for the new birth was the gateway into eternal life with God. But the moderates saw no reason why the revivals should jeopardize the social position of ministers. At every turn the moderates reviled, ridiculed, and "regulated" (to use Dickinson's word) radical excesses.

The most prominent radical leader, James Davenport, provided an easy target for the moderates' and antirevivalists' attacks. Davenport's emotional preaching style reached popular audiences more effectively than almost anyone else's, save perhaps for Whitefield's. But Davenport more self-consciously sought out the poor and the outcast of society than did Whitefield or most moderate evangelicals. Newspaper reports scoffed at how Davenport led crowds of the disenfranchised singing through the streets. He made more inroads among Native Americans in New England than any of his white evangelical contemporaries. He also proved the most willing to challenge the salvation of established ministers, and he raised funds for an alternative college, the Shepherd's Tent of New London, Connecticut, which drew away Yale students who wanted an education in evangelical piety and preaching. In 1742 Connecticut legislators passed an anti-itinerancy law specifically designed to catch Davenport as its first quarry. Deported from Connecticut, Davenport made his way to Boston, where he declared a number of ministers unconverted, including several moderate evangelical leaders. He was arrested, but at the trial he was declared non compos mentis and released. Psychological diagnoses are difficult to make at a distance of two and a half centuries, but Davenport was almost certainly not mentally ill. He was just the key leader of New England's evangelical radicals.

Davenport came to believe that he went too far in the dramatic episode that has defined his career: a 1743 book-and-clothes burning on the wharf in New London. Davenport called on the crowd to burn books, not only by antirevivalist authors but also by moderate evangelicals who supported the awakenings. Taking a stab at elite fashion, Davenport also called on the crowd to burn all their "affected finery," and he committed his own pants as fuel for the fire. When it came to burning clothes, his supporters balked and realized that Davenport had crossed a line of propriety. The humiliated Davenport immediately began working to resurrect his ruined pastoral career, blaming the debacle on a feverish daze that the devil seized upon to lead him into enthusiastic madness.

After Davenport's bonfire incident, moderate churches, colonial governments, and hostile publications began to turn against the radicals in force. When George Whitefield returned to America in 1744, he defended himself against charges that he had created the chaos of the awakenings. Davenport and Whitefield both realized that they needed to cast themselves as moderates in order to salvage their careers. Davenport had farther to go, but he successfully won back the favor of most moderate evangelicals by abandoning his strident populist style. Whitefield stopped questioning the salvation of established ministers, adopted a less-confrontational manner, and became a religious favorite again across the colonies. The remaining radicals found that they had to start their own churches, which in the New England colonies was illegal. The new Separate Congregational churches of New England reflected an institutionalization of the radical impulse. Many Separates, seeking an even-purer church model, decided to become Baptists. They concluded that Congregational churches were impure primarily because they baptized infants, giving the unconverted children pseudomemberships in the church.

Many of those baptized babies never experienced the new birth. Returning to what they saw as the original model of the New Testament, the Baptists only baptized converted believers, as a sign of their entrance into the pure church of saints. The evangelical Baptists also carried on the radical tradition through the 1750s and 1760s as they sent many missionaries into the backcountry south, helping to begin the long transformation of that benighted region into the Bible Belt.

In the light of this new understanding of the contested origins of American evangelicalism, how should we understand the significance and scope of the Great Awakening? Until 1982 historians unquestioningly assumed the existence and importance of the Great Awakening, but then historian Jon Butler brought the whole colonial-history narrative into question by arguing in a seminal *Journal of American History* article that the "Great Awakening" was an "interpretative fiction" invented by nineteenth-century Christian historians. Butler dismantled all previous assumptions about the Awakening. For instance he asserted that the Awakening really only amounted to a brief Calvinistic revival in New England. While the evidence suggests that the revivals' effects extended further and lasted longer than Butler allowed, his criticism certainly made historians look more carefully at what the Great Awakening actually was.

In order to demonstrate the significance of the Great Awakening as more than an interpretive fiction, I want to discuss two of Butler's key points of attack. First he argued that the revivals had little effect on the status of colonial religion and that their implications were "never radical." I would contend that the Great Awakening dramatically changed the nature of colonial religion by forming American evangelicalism, a new elaboration of Christian faith that heavily emphasized the Holy Spirit's work in creating revivals and the individual's experience of the "new birth." That development alone makes the Great Awakening a monumental event in the course of American and world history.[2]

More specifically it is clear that the Great Awakening had all kinds of radical implications, both religiously and socially. Butler's critique does help us to see that we should not view the evangelical movement as a homogeneous unit. Moderate leaders supported the spiritual effects of the revivals while trying to restrain their social disruptions, but radicals believed that the season of grace opened a new kind of spiritual democracy, with women, African Americans, Native Americans, the uneducated, and children all taking more prominent roles in churches. One might criticize evangelical leaders for taking no action on the issue of slavery, and figures like Edwards, Whitefield, and

Davenport even owned slaves. However the radical implications of evangelical piety for slave owning bore fruit in the Revolutionary era, as many of Edwards's disciples (including his own son, Jonathan Edwards Jr.) became antislavery advocates. Most early African American critics of slavery were also evangelicals.

Evangelical radicalism also bolstered the move for disestablishment of state churches, which typically began with the evangelicals' fight to be protected from persecution as dissenters. Separates and Baptists in New England, along with Presbyterians and Baptists in Virginia, faced harassment from established church authorities and the state. In the 1750s these dissenters began to call on the provincial governments to stop giving any denomination preferential treatment. These efforts transformed in the 1770s into full-blown disestablishment campaigns, which were supported in every case by evangelicals, especially those of a more radical bent. The momentum for passing Thomas Jefferson's Statute for Establishing Religious Freedom (1786) depended heavily on Jefferson and James Madison's evangelical colaborers. Similarly, in South Carolina, evangelical Presbyterian William Tennent III led the effort for disestablishment. Perhaps the evangelicals' most heroic work for disestablishment came in Massachusetts, where Isaac Backus and the Baptists failed to win full religious freedom but successfully illuminated the hypocrisy of the Patriots' calls for freedom in colonies that did not afford liberty to religious minorities. Disestablishment, nationally enshrined in the First Amendment, made way for the celebrated spiritual democracy of the early republic. Contrary to Nathan O. Hatch's thesis in *The Democratization of American Christianity* (1989), however, evangelicalism did not require the Revolution to supply its democratic impulse. That tendency existed in radical evangelicalism from the movement's outset.[3] If the Great Awakening forged the early evangelical movement, gave disenfranchised people previously unimaginable religious and social roles, began to undermine the moral legitimacy of American slavery, and called into question the integrity of state-supported ministers and churches, then can we not say that its effects were transformative and radical?

I have some sympathy for a second point of Butler's attack on the significance of the Great Awakening: its supposed connection to the American Revolution. Butler argued that this connection was essentially nonexistent. Although the relationship between the Great Awakening and Revolutionary-era disestablishment seems clear, otherwise it is very difficult to show any causal relationship between the Great Awakening and the American Revolution. Although a majority of them seem to have become Patriots, American evangelicals responded in a variety of ways to the Revolution, with some becoming Loyalists or attempting to remain neutral. Nevertheless, the evidence for evangelicalism's indirect role in preparing America for the Revolution is compelling. Historians such as Gordon S. Wood have agreed that the Awakening, as a "massive defiance of traditional authority," provided an important precedent for America's challenge to the intimidating power of the British empire and the king.[4] Others have shown that the Great Awakening shaped a new, popular rhetorical style adapted by leading nonevangelical Patriots such as Patrick Henry and Thomas Paine. Evangelicals also sacralized the republican ideology that propelled the Revolution, helping to make its suspicion of power and sanguine view of liberty persuasive to Americans who refracted the decision to revolt through biblical categories.[5]

Although it did not cause the American Revolution, in most other ways it is difficult to overstate the Great Awakening's significance in American history. It created a social environment more ready for popular uprising against state power. It directly catalyzed the move toward disestablishment of the state churches. It birthed the evangelical movement in America, which continues to exercise great influence in national politics and expand its reach across the globe. From its origins, however, American evangelicalism was deeply conflicted, exhibiting signs both of social conservatism and of radical egalitarianism. To the extent that America has become highly religious, pluralistic, egalitarian, and fractious, the First Great Awakening surely deserves some of the credit.

Notes

1. Jonathan Dickinson, *Christian History,* October 8, 1743, 256; Jonathon Parson, *Christian History,* July 21, 1744, 73; *Christian History,* July 23, 1743, 161–66.

2. Jon Butler, "Enthusiasm Described and Decried: The Great Awakening as Interpretative Fiction," *Journal of American History* 69 (1982): 323.

3. Nathan O. Hatch, *The Democratization of American Christianity* (New Haven, Conn.: Yale University Press, 1989), 5–7.

4. Gordon S. Wood, "Religion and the American Revolution," in *New Directions in American Religious History,* ed. Harry S. Stout and D. G. Hart (New York: Oxford University Press, 1997), 182.

5. Harry S. Stout, "Religion, Communications, and the Ideological Origins of the American Revolution," *William and Mary Quarterly,* 3d ser., 34 (1977): 519–41; Mark A. Noll, "The American Revolution and Protestant Evangelicalism," *Journal of Interdisciplinary History* 23 (1993): 615–38.

Can Jonathan Edwards (and His Heirs) Be Integrated into the American History Narrative?

George Marsden

Jonathan Edwards is widely acknowledged as the most impressive intellect in early America, and he is often ranked as America's greatest theologian. In addition his practical work in fostering evangelical awakenings places him near the fountainhead of one of the most influential popular movements in American culture.

Despite such stature both in elite and popular culture, Edwards typically appears as a tiny blip in general accounts of American history. Although he gets a respectful paragraph in the better college survey texts, if the general public remembers him at all, it is almost solely for his terrifying sermon, "Sinners in the Hands of an Angry God." The effect is that to the extent that Edwards is remembered, it is to dismiss him as representing an outlook that a later, more tolerant America has thankfully escaped.

The problem is an instance of the larger one of how to deal with exclusivist religion in telling the story of America. People who believe that their religious views are correct and that all other views are dangerously wrong just do not seem to fit in. Even though it is easily demonstrable that such religion has had a major impact in shaping the experience of countless Americans, and hence it is important just for *understanding* American history, it is easier to ignore, marginalize, or caricature, since the impact runs counter to a dominant master narrative of diversity and tolerance. Valuable as these latter ideals unquestionably are, R. Laurence Moore in *Religious Outsiders and the Making of Americans* (1986) pointed out the historical problem with this approach alone. In telling of the Catholic experience in America, for instance,

From *Historically Speaking* 5 (July/August 2004)

the most typical story line has been a Whiggish tale of the triumph of Americanist Catholics over retrograde conservatives. In broader tellings of American history, even such subtleties as this may be lost. While religion's prominent role in shaping immigrant communities may be mentioned, the potentially controversial subjects of substantive religious teachings, their cultural impacts, and tensions concerning them are likely to be ignored. Issues of class and race (as in "whiteness studies") are more likely to be emphasized.

The most prominent exception to this rule is the Puritan religion of seventeenth-century New England. The importance of such exclusivist belief is too evident to ignore, and ever since the era of Perry Miller, Puritan studies have been sophisticated enough to take the new Englander's outlook seriously and often sympathetically. Nonetheless in recent decades the imperative to emphasize diversity has displaced Puritanism from any priority it once held. In teaching about the early settlements, as many other voices as possible must be given equal time regardless of long-term cultural influences. While there is value in recognizing that most of colonial America was far different from New England and especially in taking seriously the roles and viewpoints of native cultures, recognition of the fundamental role of Protestantism in shaping (for good or for ill) subsequent American culture is ultimately diminished.

Such diminishment becomes more pronounced in the accounts of the eighteenth century just about when Edwards makes his appearances in historical narratives. Here there is no escaping the influence of George Whitefield and the Great Awakening (with a mention of Edwards) as the first colonial-wide popular event, but then the narrative moves quickly to the American Revolution and politics. After that the story of religion in America gives way to the implicit motif of steady secularization. Religion's role in the opposition to slavery is acknowledged, but otherwise it appears largely as a rearguard phenomenon, as in anti-Catholicism, Prohibition, fundamentalism, and the rise of the religious Right. Paradoxically the actual development of religion in American history is nearly opposite to the standard secularization story. Exclusivist forms of Christianity and other faiths seem to become *more popular* as the nation modernizes. More precisely, even as many aspects of public culture become more secular and profane, exclusivist religion flourishes as a more-or-less private option (but often with significant public implications). American culture is both remarkably religious and remarkably secular. The failure of the American educational establishment to provide perspective for understanding exclusivist religion in our midst is surely one reason why so many Americans have difficulty fathoming the dynamics of exclusivist religion abroad.

What does this all have to do with Edwards? Because American historians (and American secular culture generally) fail to take evangelical religion seriously, many well-educated people are mystified by its persistent strength. The standard secularization story simply does not account for actual American experience. Sociologists in recent decades have pointed out the inadequacy for American history of the paradigm of inexorable secularization. Most historians, however, persist in working with the older secularization story that became canonical in the Progressive era. If we are to present an alternative story that takes evangelicalism seriously as one of the major and most remarkable components shaping the American experience, then the restoration of Edwards as a major figure—a spiritual founding father—is one important step. Other figures, Whitefield for instance, may be equally or more important. Attention to Edwards, however, points out that one is dealing with a movement that is not *just* popular but that also has had an intellectual-spiritual component with deep roots and long-lasting implications in shaping wider American culture, especially in the era before the Civil War. In the history of higher education, for instance, Edwards's New England heirs (even if not all strict Edwardseans) shaped many of the most influential schools. Many American foreign missions began under similar auspices. The larger cultural vision also had political implications. Harriet Beecher Stowe and John Brown were each shaped by Edwardsean religious sensibilities. John M. Murrin's provocative counterfactual speculation states the case most dramatically: "Without the Great Awakening and its successors, there would have been a revolution in 1775, but in all probability, no Civil War in 1861."[1]

While Edwards is hardly representative of the entire evangelical movement that followed, he does articulate some of its central themes. Perhaps most significant is Avihu Zakai's approach, presented in *Historically Speaking* and in *Jonathan Edwards's Philosophy of History: The Reenchantment of the World in the Age of Enlightenment.*[2] Edwards, who was consciously countering Enlightenment trends to define history in terms of human agency alone, argued that God's work in religious awakenings was the true center of human history. A postmillennialist and in some ways a man of his times in his historical optimism, Edwards believed that before long, probably by 2000 A.D., all of human culture would be transformed through worldwide revival. After that would come a golden age of a thousand years when the human population would be soaring geometrically, and almost everyone would be converted.

Whatever our personal views of this scenario, it is historically important for understanding influential visions of history and of the purpose of life that differ markedly from Enlightenment and post-Enlightenment views. Such outlooks have inspired countless Americans and untold numbers abroad. Although this world view comes in many varieties, anyone who professes to know something about American popular culture should be familiar at least with its main themes. For the past century its premillennial versions (Christ comes before the golden age) have been prevalent. The immense bestselling popularity of the *Left Behind* book series by Tim LaHaye and Jerry Jenkins is only the latest manifestation of a cultural phenomenon that few American cultural historians have the resources to explain. More important than the details of such popularizations is a view of history expressed in them that has a lot more to do with popular evangelical behavior than do their specific end-time scenarios. For dedicated evangelicals redemption is at the center of history and of life. That means that the overriding consideration in human relationships is the salvation of otherwise lost souls. Why else have so many missionaries risked the lives of themselves and their families? How else do we account for Bible believers' relentless evangelism of their neighbors? We do not have to like this outlook, and as historians we can see that a lot more is involved than the expressed beliefs; but we do need to recognize how such views help shape the personal, social, and political behavior of many Americans.

Once we recognize the continuing cultural significance of the popular forms of the movement, we still face the issue of how to take it seriously as a force in American history. Studying the market-driven popular forms is essential, but that is only part of the picture and can reinforce the stereotypical tendency of outsiders to dismiss the movement. It is like looking only at McDonald's to understand the history of American restaurants. Or, perhaps a little more precisely, it is like looking only at the vapid rhetoric of contemporary American politicians to understand American politics while ignoring the founding fathers. If one is to appreciate how evangelicalism developed such deep roots in American soil, one should not treat it as though it is essentially a recurrent reactionary movement driven by religious hucksters. Students should learn not only of "the democratization of American religion," which Nathan O. Hatch so compellingly describes, but also of at least the rudiments of the intellectual bases for the emergence of "America's God," as Mark A. Noll's recent volume of that title suggests.[3] Edwards thus would gain a significant place in the narrative.

Joseph A. Conforti has aptly observed that Edwards is "a kind of white whale of American religious history."[4] Telling the story of America without its most influential religion and without Edwards is arguably like *Moby-Dick* without the whale.

Integrating Edwards into our histories as a founding father of one of America's most popular movements has the added advantage that Edwards was a profound thinker from whom people of many persuasions might learn. For students of evangelical heritage, Edwards can be a model for strengthening their understanding and appreciation of their own traditions. First he is a counter to the anti-intellectualism sometimes associated with that heritage. Further Edwards's analysis of true and false religious affections in the Great Awakening dealt with many of the tendencies that later became dominant in many forms of evangelicalism. Edwards insisted that religious experience must be thoroughly God centered, as most evangelicals would agree it should be. Yet, having learned from hard experience, Edwards pointed out that much religious enthusiasm can be a celebration of one's own euphoria. Being in love with one's own experience can easily be mistaken for loving God, and the former fails to lead to long-term sacrificial commitment.

In teaching about Edwards, one useful device is to contrast his outlook of finding meaning in a God-centered universe with Benjamin Franklin's celebration of the autonomous self. Franklin's down-to-earth practicality is more immediately attractive to most people and has had wider influence in shaping American culture. One can point out, for instance, how much Franklin's ideals have influenced even the heirs of Edwards. American evangelicalism has often lapsed into a gospel of self-fulfillment, success, and a way to wealth. Even when it is not so corrupted, it tends to adopt Franklinesque practical traits of simple formulas, scientific calculations, and easy steps to reach one's goals. Such pragmatism is by no means all bad, and it doubtless is one key to American evangelical resilience, a trait that it would have lacked had it strictly followed the often-inflexible Edwards. Recognizing such complexities in the heritage is important for any sophisticated appreciation of its dynamics.

For those concerned with broader American history, the contrast between Edwards and Franklin suggests the issue of considering alternatives to the Enlightenment "can do" optimism that has prevailed in most of American culture. From foreign policy to the world of advertising, Americans are surrounded by assertions that there should be virtually no limits, given the right combination of self-interested determination, good will, and know-how. Americans accordingly have difficulty recognizing any contradiction between their own interests and the welfare of others, whether in considering the welfare of other nations or of the poor at home. They have, in short, inherited the teachings of the Scottish Enlightenment (and of founders such as Franklin), which hold that self-interested humans have a natural capacity to obtain "true virtue"—a belief that Edwards argued was inherently problematic.

More broadly the contrast between Edwards and the Enlightenment provides an opportunity to introduce the issue of the impact of optimistic views of human nature on American history. Enlightenment versions of such views have been reinforced by romanticism, progressivism, pragmatism, and the consumer culture of advertising. Edwards argued that human confidence in our abilities to solve our problems on our own is an illusion based on the false belief that humans are naturally good or at least not so bad that our faults could not be largely corrected by wise social arrangements. On the one hand, we can give due credit to such Enlightened optimism for its many social and political achievements. On the other hand, Edwards and his ilk provide an important counterpoint that should temper the optimistic illusions to which our culture, especially with today's hype, is prone. The unmatched social progress of the twentieth century was accompanied by unmatched atrocities. As has been often remarked, the traditional Christian doctrine that has been best supported by empirical evidence is the doctrine of original sin. As Reinhold Niebuhr so eloquently observed, realism regarding the indelible flaws in human nature can be a great asset for self-understanding, whether it be for individuals, interest groups, or nations.

Even if we can translate Edwards's tightly argued ideas into concepts that college sophomores can understand, the greatest obstacle to integrating Edwards into American history for diverse audiences is that he was a Christian theologian. On this point I think the approach of Perry Miller is a helpful place to start. Miller argues that Edwards should be studied simply because he was one of America's most profound thinkers, a great artist who happened to work in the medium of ideas.[5] That argument, so far as it goes, provides a good public basis for paying attention to Edwards. If Ralph Waldo Emerson, who was also essentially a theologian, is worth studying, then so is Edwards. Yet Miller's approach also diminishes Edwards. Edwards was indeed a great artist, but he was first of all a theologian working in a very particular religious tradition. The particularity of the tradition simply needs to be acknowledged, even if it does not fit the modern and postmodern grand narratives of inclusivism. In order to understand American history, one has to understand that huge numbers of Americans have been profoundly shaped by particularistic theological heritages, whether they be Catholic, evangelical, Orthodox Jewish, Mormon, Islamic, or many others. These need to be understood on their own terms. Especially important for understanding larger cultural trends is a religious tradition such as Calvinism, which has maintained such large influences on other dimensions of American life.

Once we get past the mistaken belief that serious talk about theology ought to be out of bounds, we can help persons of all persuasions to appreciate the alternative that Edwards's theological vision provides in contrast to the Enlightenment and to more prevalent American outlooks. First, of course, we must explain the basics of hard-nosed, biblically literalistic Reformed Christianity, some aspects of which persons of contemporary sensibilities may find off-putting. Beyond that, however, we can point out Edwards's creativity in marshaling the resources of that tradition. Particularly illuminating in my view is that in contrast to the Enlightenment/Deist tendency to distance God from creation and to foster a depersonalized universe, Edwards insisted that the starting point for all thought must be the recognition that the universe is essentially personal. All being originates in the interpersonal relationships of the Trinity, and the very purpose of creation is to express God's redemptive love. Hence all of created reality is a text or language about the love and beauty of God, epitomized ultimately in the sacrificial love of Christ for the undeserving. In all that is around them, whether in stunning landscapes, ordinary objects, or other people, believers can see the beauty of a loving God revealed as "Images, or Shadows, of Divine Things." Those who are, through God's grace, given the eyes to see that beauty in Christ are inexorably drawn to it so that they desire to love what God loves, or all that is good.

Edwards's outlook contrasts to most American alternatives in that he weds beauty to practicality. In our instrumental-technological culture, we tend to divorce the two, seeing beauty as a relief from the dreariness and impersonality of our mundane, task-oriented activities. For Edwards the overwhelming beauty of God's love in Christ is at the very center of reality. Not everyone will be pleased by this Edwardsean vision. Many heirs to Franklin will find it repelling and will prefer the down-to-earth practicality of enlightened self-interest tempered by civic consciousness. Whether one likes the Edwardsean vision or not, however, if we are speaking historically, we need at least to take it seriously as a profound articulation of an ideal that has transformed countless lives and leavened many dimensions of human experience.

Notes

1. John M. Murrin, "No Awakening, No Revolution? More Counterfactual Speculations," *Reviews in American History* 11 (1983): 169.

2. Avihu Zakai, "Jonathan Edwards's Vision of History," *Historically Speaking: The Bulletin of the Historical Society* 4 (June 2003): 28–30. *Jonathan Edwards's Philosophy of History: The Reenchantment of the World in the Age of Enlightenment* (Princeton, N.J.: Princeton University Press, 2003).

3. Nathan O. Hatch, *The Democratization of American Christianity* (New Haven, Conn.: Yale University Press, 1989); Mark A. Noll, *America's God: From Jonathan Edwards to Abraham Lincoln* (New York: Oxford University Press, 2002).

4. Joseph A. Conforti, *Jonathan Edwards, Religious Tradition, and American Culture* (Chapel Hill, N.C.: University of North Carolina Press, 1995), 1.

5. Perry Miller, *Jonathan Edwards* (New York: Sloane, 1949), v.

Comment on Marsden

Bruce Kuklick

To much of what Professor Marsden has written, I can only say, "Amen," which I hope he will appreciate. At the same time I think the problems of a diminished religious history are not so bad as he believes, and would also suggest that his conceptualization of these problems is a little one-sided.

Many people have called for a revival of American religious history, and there is even some discussion of it in the high-level "Interchange" among several prominent historians in the September 2003 issue of the *Journal of American History.* Indeed, I thought that the "New Religious History," as exemplified in the work of Robert Orsi, was well underway. Marsden might be a bit uncomfortable with the focus on popular religion and the anthropological slant given to its study, but this is still a healthy sign for all of us who justifiably recognize how religious belief—and certainly the kind of belief that Marsden calls "exclusivist"—has been an important and enduring component of American history.

So my own call to study our religious history would not be as strong as Marsden's. There are many claims on students, and religious history has not recently been without effective advocates or practitioners.

I also think Marsden's approach to the subject may do historians a disservice. For a very long time New England Puritanism was at the beginning and then the center of American history. And for a very long time historians acknowledged this in an uncritical way. The great nineteenth-century narrators of American life—Bancroft, McMaster, and Parkman—gave prominence to exclusivist Protestantism and read the American experience as if it were imbued with this Protestantism. In the very recent past synthetic interpreters of our international engagements have recognized the influence of religion in the secular sphere, using such terms as righteous empire, manifest destiny, promised land, and crusader state when depicting the role of the United States in the world.

Marsden finds it useful to juxtapose Benjamin Franklin with Jonathan Edwards as a way of broadening the secularist tilt of historians who have ignored the importance of religion. Examining the contrast between Edwards and Franklin, says Marsden, would enable such historians to see how the concerns for which Edwards stood have colored American history. But contrasting the two is an old and conventional trope in American Studies. Carl Van Doren's *Franklin and Edwards: Selections* dates from 1920. Van Doren clearly sides with the "victorious" Franklin and Van Doren inaugurated a popular twentieth-century tradition of illuminating the American character by commenting on the two men, their epigones, and the influence of their competing ideas in American life. Walter Isaacson's recent bestseller *Benjamin Franklin* (2003) takes up the identical competition.

The trouble is that this comparison is too limiting, and that in part is why religious history went into a decline. One does not have to be a historical interpreter of genius to recognize that the focus on Franklin and Edwards is constrained in telling us about the experience of Native Americans, women, African Americans, or Euro-Americans who did not come from Northwest Europe. In the last thirty years especially, these hitherto-muffled voices have come into their own and, in the profession, crowded out white males like Edwards and Franklin. But Marsden writes as if it were ever thus, and it wasn't. One could argue that as an organizing principle Protestantism had a good run for its money but lost out because it was unable to interpret new themes that began to capture the interest of historians. Marsden is correct to intimate that religious history has much to offer even these newer areas of inquiry and needs again to be brought to the forefront of our understanding. But the operative word here is *again:* Marsden sometimes writes as if historians had never attended to religion; they did and still do today more than he admits.

The real issue for Marsden is that he might not like it when he gets what he wants, as he surely will: religious history, I am convinced, will make even more of a comeback than it already has. But Marsden envisages that it should use a somewhat-rarified set of suppositions from intellectual history whereby Edwards's ideas get played out in popular culture, as in Joseph Conforti's *Jonathan Edwards, Religious Tradition, and American Culture* (1995). Brace yourself! When the New Religious History gets into gear, it may well treat the postmedieval Biblical worldview of Edwards as an anthropologist would treat an early cargo cult. Edwards's "reenchantment" of the world and his "postmillennialism" may look far different to the future religious historians that he yearns for than these beliefs look to Marsden himself.

There is one final aspect of Marsden's hope for a new religious history that bears comment. When he writes about religious exclusivists, he mainly means

Protestant exponents of the Covenant of Grace, and he emphasizes their affinity with the strand in Edwards that stresses humility and walking modestly with one's God. Marsden suggests that a new religious history will accentuate the beliefs of a Christian America at odds with the materialism and aggrandizement so troubling to reflective students of our national past. This humility is undoubtedly part of the Edwardsean approach, but Marsden underestimates the other aspect of this approach that provides room for self-assertion and self-righteousness in the Calvinist dialectic of self-abasement and self-assurance. Anyone who doubts this fact need only read Edwards's "Farewell Sermon" to his Northampton parish or "Sinners in the Hands of an Angry God," which is certainly not all of Edwards but cannot be dismissed completely, as the theologian's most sophisticated interpreters have recently tended to do.

Take the area of war making, which I know best. Walking humbly with one's God did not deter Abraham Lincoln from unleashing on the United States the most destructive war in its history. The great Presbyterian Woodrow Wilson was more arrogant than any other president in American history, and his actions had dubious consequences for the world in the twentieth century. Cold War Protestants who determined to shape the world abound: Truman, Acheson, Dulles, Rusk, Nixon, Carter, and surely George W. Bush. These are not men known for their meekness; they are rather men such as Edwards, who was certain that his enemies were instruments of the devil.

It occurs to me that Marsden is trying to imply that we would have had a kinder and gentler America were the Edwardsean outlook—in contrast to the Franklinian one that has been somewhat more prevalent—to have been even more pervasive in American history than it has been. If this supposition about Professor Marsden turns out to be true, a new religious history may well surprise him.

Completion or Revision

Wilfred M. McClay

I would like to begin by expressing my enormous gratitude to George Marsden for all he's done to expand and challenge our sense of what American historical writing is and what it could be. I know that in saying such things I speak for many others, and I'm hardly the first to say them. But they still need to be said, and acknowledgment needs to be made of the courage, generosity, and gentle tenacity he's shown in pressing these issues, constantly seeking fresh ways of articulating his concerns. He could have played it safe, the way most of us do. There's no doubt that he would be ranked one of the outstanding historians of his generation solely on the basis of his superb work in American religious history, ranging from his foundational early studies of evangelicalism and fundamentalism to his extraordinary new biography of Jonathan Edwards. Why then complicate matters by venturing out into the murky and unpredictable waters of theory, where so many promising enterprises seem to lose their way?

Well, for whatever reason, he has not been content to hug the shore. Having established himself through his scholarship as, so to speak, a Hebrew of Hebrews, a professional historian beyond reproach, he has elected to "use his tenure" to raise provocative questions about the limitations of his profession and explore the possibility of a more intimate and holistic relationship between religious conviction and historical scholarship. I doubt that anyone else could have raised these questions with the same credibility. Lesser scholars who have sought to infuse their religious commitments into the process of writing history have found themselves quickly (and often quite deservedly) pushed to the margins. But it is much harder to dismiss a historian with George Marsden's massive accomplishments, particularly when he has sought

From *Historically Speaking* 5 (July/August 2004)

to treat his own explorations of the integration of faith and scholarship not merely as a personal matter but as an undertaking with wider significance for the entire profession.

Still his principal contention—that self-consciously "Christian scholarship" should not be regarded as an "outrageous idea"—is far from having carried the day, even among Christian scholars. From the beginning it has caught prodigious flak from all sides: from mainstream secular thinkers who believe that the de-Christianization of the American academy is one of the twentieth century's greatest achievements; from scholars who happen to be privately Christian but are entirely content to keep the spheres of religion and scholarship rigorously separate—they have made their careers that way and are thoroughly uncomfortable with the idea of fooling with the status quo; and, from a very different direction, hostile fire comes from postsecular thinkers, Christian and otherwise, as well as some religious conservatives, who find Marsden's goal of seeking a "place at the table" for religiously informed scholarship too timid, precisely because it buys into too many of the outmoded Enlightenment-project rules of the game, rules that these writers believe to be hopelessly problematized and compromised. Other more traditionally minded scholars are similarly dissatisfied with Marsden's propositions but for opposite reasons. Many would like to see a more full-throated defense of Judeo-Christianity's foundational place in the enterprise of scholarship, as the original and unacknowledged "host" of the dinner party. And nearly all are made uneasy by Marsden's resort to the strategy of multiculturalism—if we are to have feminist scholarship, gay scholarship, disability scholarship, and the like, then why not Christian scholarship? But such a move, they feel, goes much too far down the fatal road of relativism and embraces the disordered pattern of contemporary scholarship at precisely the point where it is weakest and most in need of reformation.

So George Marsden's theoretical explorations have supplied target practice for a lot of people. But if one's influence can be measured by the number of interesting arguments one starts and the number of thoughtful reconsiderations one induces, his efforts have not been in vain. In any event he continues on undaunted, and the present essay is only the latest installment in a quest that has been underway for at least a decade now, going back to the publication of his *Soul of the American University* (1994). In that work he argued that by the middle of the twentieth century, the Protestant orthodoxy that dominated American higher education for three centuries had been decisively dethroned, only to be replaced by a new, if unacknowledged, orthodoxy of unbelief. Although Marsden showed no nostalgia for the old ways, he was unhappy with the new ones, which imposed their own intellectual coercions and impoverishments, stifling free religious expression and bracketing off whole dimensions of human thought and experience. Surely, he reflected, there was a better way to go about the business of scholarship.

But the exact shape of that better way has proven elusive and not least for historians. Is the better way merely a matter of supplementing and correcting the existing master narrative by reinserting the religious history that a secular-minded profession has sought to leave out? Or does it mean challenging the whole explanatory structure of mainstream historiography from top to bottom, questioning hierarchies of meaning, questioning what counts as a cause or an agent, questioning the fact/value distinction, questioning the very possibility of scholarly objectivity or disinterestedness, questioning what is meant by "progress," questioning the relationship between secular events and transcendental realities—and thereby questioning the very premises that led to the erasure of religious perspectives in the first place?

There are considerable differences between these possibilities, and Marsden himself is not always clear which of them he's talking about. Such is the case in the essay at hand. Should we dramatically increase our attention to Edwards in standard accounts of American history in order to complete the picture and fill in elements missing from the master narrative? Or should we radically revise the existing narrative, even jettison it, and devise an entirely new one? Should we seek completion or radical revision? One is reminded of some of the debates among exponents of women's history between those who sought to add stories of women to the existing narratives and those who sought to transform the entire discipline and the disciplinary master narratives with it in the image of their own subdisciplinary insights. Something of the same dilemma is present here. Most of the time Marsden seems merely to be advocating that Edwards be allotted more space in the existing narrative. But other times he seems to suggest that the narrative itself is the problem, as in its inability to account for the persistence and steady growth of "exclusivist" religion in modernizing America.

What is most interesting to me, however, is the fact that Marsden seems not to question that we require some kind of master narrative and insists only that we need to include Edwards in it, in a manner proportionate to his importance. Indeed this essay seems to me ultimately a call for a better and more accurate American master narrative, one truer to the genuine pluralism of American life and more resistant to the absolute hegemony of the secularization story. But my point is that Marsden is very much interested in influencing the larger picture. There is more going on here than mere jostling for a place at the table. That intention is signaled repeatedly by his choice of words. He seeks "the restoration of Edwards as a major figure" and "a spiritual founding father," part of a movement profoundly affecting "wider American culture," shaping "the most influential schools" and "the larger cultural vision"—not to mention such signal events as the American Civil War! Edwards provides "an important counterpoint" to the quasi-official optimism of American culture.

All this is right and important. But a "counterpoint" is a completion or elaboration of an existing form, not a radical revision of it. And if one is really going to challenge the primacy of the secularization story, one has to offer something in its place. Which is not to say that the "counterpoint" image is not a good one. It is certainly valuable to point out that there have been, and still are, plenty of Americans who reject the premises of Enlightened optimism and embrace the tenets of particularistic and supernaturalist religion. And it is helpful and responsible to point out that well-educated Americans ought to know of such things, even if they reject such beliefs themselves. But it is a very different matter to assert, or even suggest, that those Americans who possess a strong religious perspective may derive a cognitive benefit thereby and may find themselves brought within range of insights that are simply not accessible to those holding to a materialist or secularist perspective.

Marsden stops short of asserting such a thing, but I wonder if he should have. One need not be giddy with the vapors of postmodernism to see, as Marsden does, that an older conception of the intellectual life, epitomized by Anselm's *fides quaerens intellectum,* has acquired a new plausibility in the postmodern era. But the hard part is knowing what to do responsibly with this insight, without allowing it to sink the entire scholarly enterprise. Here one thinks of the more adventurous (if tentative) aspects of Marsden's earlier work on the distinctiveness of Christian scholarship and the possible forms of scholarly community in which it might thrive. One wonders what these explorations might contribute to the present instance. What if one were to experiment with an entirely different starting point? What if, for example, this essay were to examine not merely whether Edwards can be integrated into the American History Narrative but also whether the American History Narrative can be integrated into the thought of Edwards?

That would be a very powerful move indeed, both as a way of challenging the secularization story and testing the true depth and significance—and present-day relevance—of Jonathan Edwards. But it is also, one must say, probably a bridge too far for the present generation of scholars, which has yet to be convinced that there can be any responsible or workable alternative to our current premises. Such reluctance seems to me justified. To poke holes in the premises of present-day scholarship and reveal its inadequate epistemological basis is pretty easy. To propose that historical writing needs to be dramatically reconceived is even easier. But it's much harder to propose a proven alternative that we can actually live by and work with both as scholars and as human beings. If that alternative case is ever to be made, it will have to be made not by clever theorists or bold manifestoes but by concrete acts of brilliant and persuasive scholarship.

Marsden's biography itself, far more powerfully than his essay, makes such a compelling case for Edwards's berth at the American table. Once that fact is admitted, then we may have an easier time of it when we begin thinking seriously about the table itself. For that task, too, we are likely to find ourselves in George Marsden's debt.

Response to McClay and Kuklick

George Marsden

I am grateful for these perceptive responses, each of which points out some ambiguities in my essay and offers the opportunity to sort out and clarify the issues.

Both respondents note some duality of purpose in my essay. On the one hand, I claim prescriptively that the study of American history would be enriched if more attention were paid to the role of exclusivist religion, of which Jonathan Edwards is a notable and particularly influential exemplar. At the same time, I also make some more normative claims. I say that if students of American history were exposed to the Edwardsean heritage, they might learn some profitable things about the nature of reality, including some useful insights that might be applied to historical study itself. Although there is nothing mutually exclusive about these two types of emphases, their presence together raises the legitimate question as to what I am really up to.

Since we are all historians, perhaps the best way to answer that question is to reflect on the origins of the essay. It grows out of that self-serving enterprise of trying to explain to people why they should care about one's book. In doing that I have imagined two audiences whom I am addressing simultaneously. First there are those who are mainly interested in American history, to whom I want to say that Edwards ought to be restored to the principal canon. The other audience is made up of those who have serious religious sensibilities. So for them I have wanted to emphasize what might be learned from the sometimes off-putting Edwards.

In adapting these thoughts to professional historians who might read this publication, I have presumed that I am speaking to an audience that is similarly divided in religious commitments. So I am grateful to the commentators

From *Historically Speaking* 5 (July/August 2004)

for helping me to clarify my dual purposes. I hope that readers will recognize that my recommendations for integrating a certain type of religious history into the field are not dependent on my normative stances. Perhaps I should not have conjoined the two purposes in one essay. Nonetheless that conjunction had the happy effect of sharpening these two responses.

Sometimes I think that Wilfred McClay has a clearer perspective on what I am doing than I myself do. He is correct, first of all, that I am not proposing a radical new narrative but only that we improve the present narrative. I think of myself as a realist and hope to provide a leaven for the profession, not to convince people to introduce a whole new paradigm. When McClay raises the prospect of an American history narrative that can be integrated into the thought of Edwards, his suggestion helps clarify exactly the problem involved in introducing a radically new (or old) standard. Edwards read history as, roughly speaking, an extension of the Old Testament, with God bringing judgments or fulfilling promises through kings and armies, as well as through the spread of the Gospel. I see no value in such an approach to American history today. For one thing we do not have the requisite prophetic revelation on which to base such interpretations. Moreover I am entirely in agreement with Kuklick's warnings about the pitfalls of appropriating such traditions for national purposes. I still do think that we can learn by *selectively* appropriating a few dimensions of such outlooks, like their critique of some aspects of Enlightenment self-confidence. Nonetheless I make that recommendation only in the context of recognizing well-known dangers of more or less equating America with ancient Israel.

I do believe (and here Bruce Kuklick is on record elsewhere as strongly disagreeing) that Christians (or other religious believers) might "derive a cognitive benefit" from their religious beliefs. Here I would correct McClay's formulation when he describes that benefit as bringing religious believers "within range of insights that are simply not accessible to those holding to a materialist or secularist perspective." Since Kuklick's objection has been against this same construction, I realize that I must underscore my response. *Deriving a cognitive benefit from a particular source does not entail that others might not derive a similar cognitive benefit from another source.* Saying that one can gain pain relief from aspirin does not imply that one cannot also gain similar relief from ibuprofen. So, for instance, in my essay I argue that historians might gain from the Edwardsean tradition an alertness to the role of human depravity as an element in historical explanation. That in no way implies that historians might not gain comparable cognitive benefits regarding human perversity from materialist or secularist perspectives—or simply from reading the newspapers. Nonetheless certain traditions—secular as well as religious—may dispose us to be more critical of the optimism concerning human abilities with which we are bombarded. Bruce Kuklick interprets my prescriptive suggestions regarding American history as essentially a call for greater recognition of the place of religion in the mainstream narrative. He correctly notes that others have been saying the same thing, and we can now add Jon Butler's helpful piece on "Jack-in-the-Box Faith: The Religion Problem in American History" in the March 2004 issue of the *Journal of American History.*

While Kuklick, Butler, and I pretty much agree that it would be a good thing if religion did not typically fade away in historians' accounts of modern America, my call is, as Kuklick recognizes, also for something more specific. I think it would be beneficial, first of all, to pay more attention to the persistence of *exclusivist* religious faiths. Second there is reason to pay a lot of attention to the persistence of *exclusivist* Protestantism, which rivals Catholicism in numbers and has a claim to be the second most influential religious tradition in American culture. The first most influential tradition has been *inclusivist* or nonsectarian Protestantism, which also deserves attention proportional to its influence (although I did not talk about that in my essay).

Most of American history until the mid-twentieth century was written by inclusivist Protestants or their somewhat-secularized heirs. They tended to speak as though the Protestant Whiggish heritage broadened and led to cultural consensus. Although early America had much hard-edged religion, in accounts of modern America the story of religious differences became largely irrelevant. The post-1960s multiculturalists were, ironically, heirs to this tradition with respect to religion. While they were overthrowing the privileging of the white male Protestant establishment, they were also following the lead of that establishment in sending a message that religions are best understood as cultural phenomena, which are all pretty much alike. Like the "Protestant/Catholic/Jew" formula of the 1950s, the message was that our society would get along best if we recognize that we all have our superficial differences, but ultimately we are pretty much alike. Studies of religious practices on an anthropological basis as essentially cultural phenomena, while often illuminating academically, reinforced the message that religious differences are not something to be taken seriously on their own terms but are essentially diverse expressions of common human and cultural impulses.

While I may be caricaturing these positions, the point is that we are doing a disservice to our students by teaching them not to take religious differences seriously. Arguably some of the naïveté of our foreign policy in the Middle

East grows out of our long-standing refusal to take other people's exclusivist religious beliefs as seriously as we should. I am not arguing, of course, that the persistence of exclusivist religion at home or abroad is generally a good thing, but I do think it would be helpful for historians to take it more seriously *on its own terms.*

So my proposal is quite different from Kuklick's representation of it as a desire to return to 1950s-style history writing in which white male Protestants reigned supreme. Even though I have written about one of the whitest, most Protestant of males, I think I gained my most illuminating insights into his life by thinking of him (thanks to the style of today) in the midst of Indians and women. Far more important I think that the inclusivist Protestant/secular consensus historiography of the 1950s generally failed to take the persistently exclusivist side of Protestantism seriously enough. Perry Miller's model for understanding seventeenth-century Puritans provided an exception. But even Miller had trouble with presenting Edwards as anything more than a great intellect and artist, and for American history after that, the historiography tends to lose sight of the many exclusivist varieties of Protestantism that persisted as major cultural forces. The public resurgence of fundamentalism and conservative evangelicalism in the later twentieth century, for instance, was largely a surprise to mainstream historians, since the literature on that was so thin.

Now there is an abundant literature on such topics, much of which does take exclusivist religion seriously on its own terms, but it remains for that literature to be integrated into the mainstream narrative. Realist that I suppose myself to be, I am not calling for a whole new paradigm but only to add such topics to the old paradigm. Nonetheless I am also enough of an optimist to hope that if the insights of such literature develop in enough areas with enough excellence, they will find their way into the mainstream. Then perhaps the old secularization paradigm will—as it already has for sociologists of religion—break down, and a new one will emerge in its place.

More Than Fluff

Protestant Revivals in the 1950s

John G. Turner

Late in 1951 the UCLA football team approached its final game of the season against archrival USC. After stumbling early in their season by losing three of their first four games, the Bruins had recovered, winning three in a row before settling for a tie against Washington. It wouldn't be a banner year, but a triumph over USC would give them a winning season and local bragging rights. Donn Moomaw, UCLA's All-American linebacker, helped the Bruins best the Trojans by returning an interception for a critical touchdown in a 21–7 victory.

Moomaw attributed his feat to prayers he offered while attending a meeting of a fledgling organization: Campus Crusade for Christ. Moomaw's girlfriend had invited him to the meeting, where he met Bill Bright, the founder of the movement. Bright invited Moomaw to attend Hollywood's First Presbyterian Church the morning after the USC game. After church Bright talked Moomaw through a series of Bible verses about sin and salvation, and the two men kneeled on Bright's living-room floor as the star athlete received Jesus Christ as his savior. Soon Moomaw became a featured speaker at Campus Crusade events at UCLA and at other Golden State colleges. He referred to Jesus Christ as his new "quarterback."

Many other UCLA gridiron stars experienced similar conversions through Campus Crusade, and they talked about their faith in similar terms. Bob Davenport, an All-American fullback, called Jesus Christ "the greatest Coach and Quarterback ever." Most of the stars on UCLA's 1954 national championship football team—nicknamed the "Eleven from Heaven"—were

From *Historically Speaking* 9 (May/June 2008)

outspoken Christians, many of whom made "decisions for Christ" under Bill Bright's influence.[1]

Jesus as "the greatest coach and quarterback ever"? A God who answers prayers with interceptions, touchdowns, and victories? It's easy for historians to make fun of the banalities of 1950s religion, as professions of religiosity in that decade provide scholars with great material. The Ideal Toy Company marketed a doll that a child could make "kneel in a praying position," and the actress Jane Russell actually called God "a livin' doll." New York's Fifth Avenue Presbyterian Church introduced "Dial-A-Prayer" for a "spiritual life in a busy day," promising "one minute of inspiration." Even as church attendance and public displays of religiosity soared and Congress added "under God" to the Pledge of Allegiance, surveys revealed that Americans knew very little about the faiths to which they ostensibly adhered. A 1951 Gallup poll claimed that 53 percent of Americans could not name even *one* of the four gospels (I suspect that many did not know the meaning of the word *gospel*). Many Americans proclaimed a vapid sort of religious pluralism. A 1958 contestant on Twentieth Century–Fox's *Sing, Boy, Sing!* proclaimed, "I think all religions are the greatest." President Dwight D. Eisenhower—born to Mennonite parents but baptized as a Presbyterian twelve days after his inauguration—proclaimed that "our government makes no sense unless it is founded in a deeply felt religious faith, and I don't care what it is."[2]

To be sure there were banal elements of 1950s religion, and these cropped up in Billy Graham's well-known crusades as well as in the more obscure meetings of Campus Crusade. Graham often invited athletes, servicemen, and actresses to his meetings in order to pique audience interest and gain a hearing for his message. He used updated music and patriotic themes for the same purpose. "We used every modern means," Graham explained, "to catch the ear of unconverted young people and then punched them straight between the eyes with the gospel." And yet Graham's preaching always included warnings about hell and straightforward discussions about salvation. His statements about hell were *not* fluffy—he read Jonathan Edwards's "Sinners in the Hands of an Angry God" to his audience during his 1949 Los Angeles crusade. Hardly unconcerned about the subsequent fate of his converts, Graham's organization expended considerable time and money developing follow-up strategies that included funneling converts into churches and arranging visitations and Bible studies. Beneath its veneer of showmanship and celebrity, the Graham campaigns were serious business.

The same was true of Bill Bright's Campus Crusade for Christ. Crusaders referred to Jesus Christ as their "best friend," their "quarterback," and their

"Head Coach." Such frivolous statements, however, obscure the fact that Campus Crusade called on students to make deep commitments to Bible study, moral living, and, most of all, personal evangelism. "I'm playing on God's varsity now," commented Moomaw upon his decision to enter the ministry. Again Moomaw's comment sounds hackneyed, but it also includes a commitment to attend seminary and forego a professional football career for the pastorate. Many of the above banalities represent not the entirety of Crusade's beliefs but rather a simple "hook" to get the attention of potential converts and gain a hearing for a more substantive message. Bright expected his staff recruits—most of whom by the 1960s were recent student converts—to tirelessly practice evangelism in return for $150 per month. Like the Billy Graham Evangelistic Association, Campus Crusade took the business of evangelism seriously, experimenting with countless methods to gain a hearing for Jesus in modern America.

Historians have erred by concentrating on the superficial aspects of postwar religion, and they have also misled their readers by emphasizing the ephemeral nature of the religious boom. By the late 1950s Elvis Presley had bumped Graham convert and country singer Stuart Hamblen off the charts, and Hollywood had grown weary of religious epics like *The Ten Commandments* and *A Man Called Peter*. Many churches started to lose members, a process that has continued unabated in several mainline denominations. The idea that the religious boom was merely a temporary blip on a longer trajectory of secularization suggests that the Graham crusades, the Oral Roberts revivals, the surge of church attendance, and the establishment of new organizations like Campus Crusade produced little or nothing of enduring value.

It would be more accurate to describe two religious booms in postwar America as a revival of religion in general and a particular revival of conservative Protestantism. The first petered out by the end of the 1950s. The revival of conservative Protestantism persisted, however. Mass stadium evangelism faded from prominence to a large degree; Graham no longer held six-week citywide crusades. Yet evangelical and Pentecostal broadcasting filled that gap. Graham's own *Hour of Decision* television program helped pioneer a path followed by Oral Roberts, Pat Robertson, and now Joel Osteen. Also a plethora of organizations founded shortly before or after the war carved out enduring places in the evangelical landscape: Young Life (1939), World Vision (1950), and Campus Crusade for Christ (1951), to name only a few examples. Campus Crusade became a worldwide movement that now boasts an annual budget of nearly $500 million. While the Presbyterians and Episcopalians began losing members, the Southern Baptist Convention and the

Assemblies of God experienced explosive growth. This evangelical or more conservative religious boom did not fade away with the rest of postwar religiosity but continued to shape American religion, culture, and politics.

At a bare minimum the revivalism of the 1950s (particularly that of fundamentalists/evangelicals like Graham) provides the necessary bridge between the Scopes Trial and the Religious Right. As scholars like Joel Carpenter have persuasively demonstrated, fundamentalists hardly disappeared after 1925, and Graham matured in a fundamentalist culture now centered in but not confined to the rural South. The postwar revivals also help explain the later political influence of evangelicalism, which did not simply appear ex nihilo with the born-again candidacy of Jimmy Carter or the success of Jerry Falwell's Moral Majority four years later.

The Religious Right would not have come into being without the continued growth and vitality of conservative Protestantism in the United States after World War II. Historians have offered various explanations for this phenomenon: evangelicals proclaim a more rigorous and sometimes countercultural moral code, nimbly use technology and popular culture, and even maintain a higher birth rate. On a more basic level, evangelicalism continued to thrive because millions of Americans made faith commitments at Billy Graham and Oral Roberts crusades, at Campus Crusade for Christ meetings, and in Southern Baptist and Assemblies of God churches. Without the postwar revivals (and their continuance in conservative Protestant churches and organizations), the Religious Right would not have the demographic clout it has wielded over the past thirty years.

One simple yet often overlooked reason for evangelicals' newfound political significance in the mid-1970s was the dramatic growth of evangelical institutions. For the most part, the key figures in the Religious Right became power brokers not because they eyed political influence (although some did) but because they established mass followings. Politicians sought Graham's approval because he was the most popular religious leader in the country, as demonstrated through his crusades. Falwell had an enormous congregation and, more important, a large television audience, as did Pat Robertson. Prior to the 1970s, few evangelical leaders—with the exception of Graham and possibly Roberts—commanded large and visible institutions that held the potential for political influence. By the mid-1970s Graham was only one part of an evangelical universe crowded with parachurch organizations, megachurches, and broadcasters. Conservative politicians, beginning in earnest with Richard M. Nixon, recognized the potential of these institutions and their leaders as a way to garner the votes of white evangelicals. Without the persistent boom of conservative Protestantism that began in the 1940s, the Religious Right as we know it would be a much more marginal movement.

There was a similar general boom of religiosity in Europe following World War II, as reflected in higher church attendance and the success of Graham's European tours. But the postwar revival of religion in Europe dissipated. Although there were flickers of evangelical renewal, Western countries—aside from the United States—did not experience the long-term and widespread growth of evangelicalism. There are many reasons for evangelicalism's much greater success in the United States, such as higher rates of suburbanization and an evangelical culture largely in tune with other American values such as patriotism, capitalism, and middle-class consumerism. In any event the surge of evangelical Christianity in America became a critical factor in the cultural and geopolitical divergence of Europe (and Canada, to a somewhat lesser degree) from the United States. There is no sizable Christian Religious Right in Western Europe—perhaps tellingly there is no longer much robust conservatism of any sort on the other side of the pond.

Religion in the 1950s included everything from converted cowboy singers to platitudes of religious pluralism and touchdowns attributed to Jesus. The revivalism of the decade deserves more serious attention, particularly in textbooks and in the classroom. Moomaw drew connections between a Campus Crusade meeting, his prayers, and a key play in a UCLA football game. Moomaw, however, later went to Princeton Seminary and became the pastor of a thriving evangelical Presbyterian church in Bel Air. One of Moomaw's congregants was Ronald Reagan, and the former All-American linebacker later gave the invocation at Reagan's first presidential inauguration. Underneath the fluff of 1950s revivalism, a significant transformation in American religion took place, one that has exerted an enormous impact on recent American politics and on the place of the United States in today's world.

Notes

1. *Los Angeles Times,* March 15, April 20, 1952; William R. Bright, "Christianity on the Campus," *American Mercury,* December 1956, 137–43.

2. J. Ronald Oakley, *God's Country: America in the Fifties* (New York: Dembner Books, 1986), 320, 324, 326; Stephen J. Whitfield, *The Culture of the Cold War* (Baltimore, Md.: Johns Hopkins University Press, 1991), 86; Jon Butler, "Jack-in-the-Box Faith: The Religion Problem in Modern American History," *Journal of American History* 90 (2004): 1370.

Evangelical Churches Crossing the Ethnic Divide

Kathleen Garces-Foley

When asked what he thought of Martin Luther King Jr.'s 1963 March on Washington, Billy Graham responded, "Only when Christ comes again will little white children of Alabama walk hand in hand with little black children."[1] Graham shared the millennial theology of most white evangelicals of his time, and while personally in favor of desegregation, he believed that much social reform was pointless. Three decades later in Atlanta, Graham would share a revival stage with Coretta Scott King and urge Christians to break down racial barriers.[2] By this time white evangelicals were ready to give integration serious consideration. The number of books promoting, describing, and analyzing how to overcome racial barriers in all areas of life, but especially in the churches, has grown copiously since the 1990s. No longer waiting for Christ's return to challenge historical patterns of ethnic and racial separation, American evangelicals have become progressive leaders in the development of multiethnic churches.

Churches across the country are talking about diversity. Many make gestures of inclusion, like changing their mission statements, but few have actually become racially diverse. A nationwide survey conducted in 2000 found that only 5.5 percent of Christian churches were multiracial, defined as having no more than 80 percent of a single racial group.[3] Yet given how long American churches have insisted on an ethnic or homogeneous church model (including the white ethnic church), the energy surrounding the emerging multiethnic-church movement is remarkable. The phenomenon among evangelicals appears to be much more than a fad, as it has parallels within Roman Catholic and mainline Protestant circles.[4] Still the ethnic-church

From *Historically Speaking* 9 (July/August 2008)

model is firmly rooted in American soil and will not be replaced easily. If the current enthusiasm translates into lasting institutions, the long-standing pattern of ethnic divisions in American churches will be seriously challenged.

While evangelical Christians attribute this institutional sea change to the power of God, there are a number of major social changes underfoot that provide fertile ground for the emergence of the multiethnic church. Demographically the United States has never been so diverse, with people of color projected to make up 50 percent of the American population by 2050. Americans today have many more opportunities for contact with people of different ethnicities than did earlier generations. The forced desegregation of schools, neighborhoods, and workplaces has also translated into attitudinal changes, though these are harder to quantify. Racism still exists, to be sure, but many Americans today have become tolerant of and even favorably inclined toward racial integration. Such attitudinal changes can be inferred from various sources: the rising rates of intermarriage, integrated social networks portrayed positively on television, and the political career of Barack Obama.

The history of race relations within American Christianity is a bleak tale of strict segregation punctuated by episodes of brief interracial experiments. The first of these episodes occurred before slavery, with the establishment of colonies where black and white indentured servants mingled freely. While slavery flourished, blacks were admitted into Christian churches under a strictly enforced racial hierarchy that spatially ensured segregation. The free expression of biracial camp meetings provided greater dignity to blacks but seldom translated into the institutional church. In the North freedmen joined white churches but rarely were treated as equals even in Methodist and Baptists circles where blacks served as preachers. Even the abolitionist Quakers found it difficult to share their pews with African Americans.[5]

The early twentieth century saw a number of interracial church experiments, such as Father Divine's Peace mission, but by far the most promising were the gatherings at Azusa Street in Los Angeles. From 1906 to 1908 the African American holiness preacher William J. Seymour gathered blacks, whites, Asians, and Latinos to pray for the blessing of the Holy Spirit through the speaking of tongues. Though bystanders found this religious practice strange, it was the mixing of races as equals that proved to be most intolerable to Americans in the early twentieth century. By the 1920s the emerging Pentecostal movement had split along racial lines into the white Assemblies of God and black Church of God in Christ. Other experiments in the 1940s were longer lasting but small in scope. Perhaps the best known of these is the Church for the Fellowship of All People in San Francisco led by Howard

Thurman. Catholic parishes also began integrating in the 1950s, sometimes voluntarily but more often by fiat and in the face of strong resistance from white parishioners.

Prompted by the unrest of the civil rights movement, churches were forced to reconsider their traditional stance against integration. Because liberal Protestants embraced social integration, they also attempted to integrate their churches. Yet in practice their churches have remained very homogeneous to this day, despite well-intentioned denominational statements of inclusion. Conservative Protestants in the South strongly opposed integration while those in the North sat on the sidelines during the civil rights marches, insisting that churches had nothing to do with politics. While most of the black civil rights activists were also theologically conservative Protestants, they clearly did not support the status quo. After King's assassination many black activists were disillusioned with the failure of the civil rights movement to make greater gains and gave up on a theological appeal to the moral conscience of white Christians. Alternatively some black activists hoped to gain the support of white evangelicals by promoting a message of racial reconciliation.

Racial reconciliation denotes a contemporary theological doctrine that all people should be united as the body of Christ. It is biblically rooted in a passage from the evangelist Paul's letter to the Galatians: "There is no longer Jew or Greek, there is no longer slave or free, there is no longer male and female; for all of you are one in Christ Jesus" (3:28). Shaped by such black leaders as John Perkins and Samuel Hines, the early racial-reconciliation movement called for both a personal confession of racism and the dismantling of social structures supporting racial injustice. White evangelicals were apathetic to calls for racial reconciliation and turned to the church-growth movement to defend the ethnic-church model. A popular church-growth book by C. Peter Wagner called *Our Kind of People* (1979) served this purpose well. Wagner argues that evangelization is accomplished more readily in ethnic churches than integrated churches for the simple fact that people prefer to be with their own kind. Wagner called this natural propensity the "homogeneous unit principle." According to this principle, churches ought to be organized along ethnic lines to make it easier to bring sinners to Christ. From the church growth perspective, integrated churches are actually an obstacle to sharing the gospel because newcomers would find the diverse setting so uncomfortable.

Until the 1990s the ethnic-church model remained normative in evangelical circles, though whites considered their churches "American" rather than "ethnic." As the number of new immigrants arriving from Africa, Latin

America, and Asia grew exponentially after 1965, more ethnic churches and parachurch ministries, such as college Bible studies, were founded, often with the financial backing of white churches. These ethnic ministries flourished especially among the children of immigrants on college campuses. The success of this work was apparent at the annual Urbana Student Mission Convention in 2000 when 44 percent of the twenty thousand young adult attendees were people of color.[6] While the evangelical subculture remains dominated by whites, by the 1990s evangelicals had become a surprisingly diverse group, and leaders began to reconsider their espousal of ethnic ministry.

Although they initially disregarded racial reconciliation, white evangelicals were promoting it in the mid-1990s. Two events in the 1990s drew national attention to the racial reconciliation cause and gave the movement the influx of energy that continues to carry it today. In a 1994 event dubbed the "Memphis Miracle," leaders of the white Pentecostal Association of North America (PANA) publicly asked the African American Pentecostal denominations for forgiveness. PANA then disbanded in order to form a new multiethnic Pentecostal organization under African American leadership. In 1995 the leadership of the National Association of Evangelicals repented for the sin of racism. Other denominational bodies, such as the Worldwide Church of God and the Southern Baptist Convention, made similar public gestures, determined to pursue racial reconciliation in their organizations.

While these public displays of repentance made big headlines, it was the Promise Keepers organization, under the leadership of Bill McCartney, that put racial reconciliation on the agenda of millions of white evangelicals. One of the seven promises of the Promise Keepers was to reach beyond racial and denominational barriers to demonstrate biblical unity. To this end Promise Keeper rallies sometimes included emotional confessions of racism and acts of repentance. The racial-reconciliation agenda now embraced by mainstream evangelicalism is not nearly as radical as the early founders of the movement intended. Promise Keepers has widely promoted an apolitical, individualized version of racial reconciliation. Missing from the mainstream version is the recognition that racism has a social reality embedded in institutional practices and personal values. Instead racism is understood as solely a personal sin, making social reforms such as affirmative action seem fruitless or menacing. Under the slogan "You can't legislate love," Christians are asked to repent of their personal racism and to form cross-racial friendships rather than fight against systematic racism.

Over the last decade a generation of young evangelicals has been exposed to the theology of racial reconciliation in Sunday schools and Bible fellowships. The racial-reconciliation mission and its application in multiethnic churches have found strong supporters among young adults raised in urban settings. Generations X and Y are the inheritors of integrated schools, affirmative-action programs, and the ideology of multiculturalism, which celebrates diversity. College groups like InterVarsity Christian Fellowship have made racial reconciliation a priority. College Bible studies influence young evangelicals and are often training grounds for future church leaders. Through their college years many young evangelicals get "convicted" of the truth of racial reconciliation. When they look for a church to join as adults, this "reconciliation generation" seeks out churches that reflect their social lives. For young, cosmopolitan evangelicals, ethnic churches are seen as at best boring and at worst implicitly racist. Unable to find many existing multiethnic churches, young evangelicals are starting their own churches designed to attract other young people who value diversity.

Not surprisingly new churches formed with an original vision to be multicultural are finding more success in reaching their goal. By advertising their vision from the launch, they can attract new members who share a commitment to racial reconciliation. Across the country these new churches are attracting cosmopolitan evangelicals of all ages eager to explore cultural diversity. Affirmative action is still anathema in evangelical circles, but churches are increasingly willing to use "intentionality" in their hiring practices as a necessary means to achieving the goal of being inclusive. In the same vein more evangelicals are paying attention to cultural assimilation and taking steps to mitigate the cultural dominance of the majority group by incorporating an assortment of cultural styles from gospel to country music in their worship services.

More than fifty years since the *Brown v. Board of Education* decision, evangelical churches are actively pursuing diversity. Though they are playing catch-up to integration in the public sphere, evangelicals insist that racial reconciliation will accomplish much more than legislated integration ever can. Like other Christian groups in the United States, they are finding it surprisingly difficult to overcome the ethnic-church model. Many Christians are attracted to the multiethnic church but are unwilling to give up their comfortable, homogeneous communities.

Notes

1. William Martin, *A Prophet with Honor: The Billy Graham Story* (New York: Morrow, 1991), 286.

2. Michael O. Emerson and Christian Smith, *Divided by Faith: Evangelical Religion and the Problem of Race in America* (New York: Oxford University Press, 2000), 64.

3. Michael O. Emerson, *People of the Dream: Multiracial Congregations in the United States* (Princeton, N.J.: Princeton University Press, 2006).

4. Kathleen Garces-Foley, "New Opportunities and New Values: The Emergence of the Multicultural Church," *Annals of the American Academy of Political and Social Science* 612 (2007): 209–24.

5. Curtiss Paul DeYoung, Michael O. Emerson, George Yancey, and Karen Chai Kim, *United by Faith: The Multiracial Congregation as an Answer to the Problem of Race* (New York: Oxford University Press, 2003).

6. "Urbana 2000 Convention Report Overview," Urbana 2000: The 19th Triennial Urbana, Student Mission Convention, University of Illinois, Champaign-Urbana, December 27–31, 2000, http://www.urbana.org/archives/2000/convention-report-8/ (accessed March 10, 2007).

PART 4

The End of History

American Millennialism

Apocalyptic Religious Movements in American History

Stephen J. Stein

America has been and remains a highly receptive environment for religious movements defined in some primary way by their apocalyptic messages. But the substance of those proclamations defies easy generalization. The apocalyptic category derives from the Greek word αποκάλυψις, meaning an "uncovering" or "revelation." Apocalyptic religious movements seek to reveal or disclose that which is hidden. The primary focus of apocalyptic revelations tends to be the future or the supposed end of things. For that reason such movements usually are preoccupied with eschatological matters. Eschatology is literally concern with the "last things." Movements laying claim to apocalyptic insight often do so on the basis of special revelations or a unique understanding of sacred texts. Such movements in America are part of a long and rich tradition in religious history extending from ancient times to the present.

America has been a fertile seedbed for such movements: some have been transplanted from abroad while others have grown out of circumstances on this continent. In the colonial era many colonists who adopted an apocalyptic religious perspective were deeply influenced by European thinkers. Puritan ministers in New England, for example, knew the eschatological writings of English Reformation theologians who attempted to unlock prophetic mysteries in the Bible with special attention to the book of Revelation, that is, "The Apocalypse of St. John." They formulated ideas about the nature and timing of the millennium, the projected thousand-year personal reign of Christ on Earth that was to precede a final judgment; the identity of the Antichrist, the figure identified as the leader of the enemies of the true church; and the significance of "signs of the times," contemporary events construed as indications that the end of earthly days was fast approaching.

From *Historically Speaking* 9 (May/June 2008)

John Cotton (1584–1652), the first minister in the First Church of Boston, insisted that his congregation admit regenerate members only, a position related to his judgment that the millennium might begin in 1655. Three members of the distinguished Mather family—all Puritan ministers—employed apocalyptic reflections throughout their lifetimes. Richard Mather (1596–1669) viewed the English Civil War as potentially leading to the end of the Antichrist's reign. Increase Mather (1639–1723) believed the return of Christ was imminent. Cotton Mather (1663–1728) was willing to set particular dates within his lifetime as the moment of Christ's return, predictions that ultimately failed to materialize and therefore disappointed. Jonathan Edwards (1703–1758), a leader of the emergent evangelical movement, spent a lifetime studying the book of Revelation. On one occasion he implied that the millennium might begin in America. In 1793 his student and friend Samuel Hopkins (1721–1803), another evangelical minister, thought that the millennium might begin in another two hundred years or so.

Virtually all Protestant clergy at the time were persuaded that the Antichrist was the pope. Anti-Catholicism was widespread, and the polemics between Protestants and Catholics made apocalyptic something more than ideology. Protestants also linked the figure of the Antichrist to other contemporary opponents. During King George's War (1744–48), an imperial struggle among European nations, many American Protestants viewed the conflict as an opportunity to defeat the forces of the Antichrist equated with the Catholic nations of France and Spain. Edwards declared the English victory at Cape Breton in Canada "a dispensation of providence, the most remarkable of its kind." Apocalyptic fervor provided ideological support for the Revolutionary cause during the American War for Independence. Samuel Sherwood (1703–1783), a Congregational minister in Connecticut, equated the beast in Revelation 13 with the British monarchy. Apocalyptic reflections were preached from pulpits and published in tracts and books. Eschatological ideas permeated Protestant circles, giving adherents a distinctive sense of place in the flow of world history.

After 1790 the new American nation provided a supportive context for existing religious communities as well as new religious movements. The First Amendment of the Constitution prohibited religious establishment on the national level and supported free exercise of religion. As a result religious communities enjoyed new opportunities for growth and expansion. Creative religious thought and diverse spiritual activity prospered. Protestant evangelicals thrived, energized by revivals and camp meetings, leading some to speculate that their successes were harbingers of a coming millennium. Ministers in the principal Protestant denominations—Congregational, Presbyterian, Baptist, and Methodist—articulated optimistic apocalyptic visions, declaring that social, economic, and political progress might inaugurate a period of unparalleled prosperity and righteousness, a version of the millennial hope historians later called "postmillennialism," because in this scheme the Second Coming of Christ follows the good times. That millennial vision informed the apocalyptic hopes of many Protestants from the mid-eighteenth into the twentieth century. Members of the Beecher family, for example, including father Lyman (1775–1863) and children Catharine (1800–1878), Edward (1803–1895), Harriet (1811–1896), and Henry Ward (1813–1887), all invested heavily in progressive social causes, including education, antislavery, and women's rights, confident they were moving history toward its eschatological goal.

Among the new apocalyptic communities that prospered in the decades before the Civil War was one with roots in England, namely, the United Society of Believers in Christ's Second Appearing, commonly known as the Shakers, founded by Ann Lee (1736–1884), an illiterate factory worker who came to America in 1774 with a handful of followers. The Shakers declared Mother Ann the Second Christ and set about establishing a community based on "Millennial Laws" mandating celibacy, equality of the sexes, communal ownership of property, and an alternative concept of family. Another imported apocalyptic movement was founded by George Rapp (1757–1847), a German of peasant background who formed a separatist community that rebelled against the state church in Germany. In the opening decade of the nineteenth century, Rapp and three hundred followers came to America, settling first in Pennsylvania and later moving to Indiana. These "Harmonists," as they became known, organized a dissenting community committed to the simple life. They looked for the beginning of the millennium in the near future. Rapp believed his community was fulfilling apocalyptic prophecies revealed in the Bible.

The most successful new religious movement that began in the years before the Civil War was the Church of Jesus Christ of Latter-day Saints, known as the Mormons, founded by the Prophet Joseph Smith (1805–1844). Smith, who translated the Book of Mormon and received revelations that addressed all kinds of issues, including likely scenarios preceding the end of time. Smith indicted the nation for its evil and saw salvation only in the ranks of Zion, the LDS community. The message of the Latter-day Saints was an apocalyptic warning to the nation; in turn, the Mormons experienced opposition and oppression, including the martyrdom of the prophet himself. The community subsequently fled to the intermountain region in the West, confident that they would be vindicated when the day of the Lord dawned. By contrast William Miller (1782–1849), a Baptist lay preacher, predicted the imminent Second Coming of Christ based on his study of biblical texts. In the 1830s he began lecturing on the subject of Christ's return. Pressured by followers Miller declared that Christ's advent would occur between March 21, 1843, and March 21, 1844. Others joined and spread the apocalyptic message through books, tracts, and revival meetings. The Millerite movement attracted substantial numbers and a great deal of public attention. When the chosen dates passed, recalculation occurred; when that date also passed, disappointment and ridicule followed.

The Civil War witnessed destruction and carnage of a magnitude that invited comparison to the battle at Armageddon, site of the projected final struggle between the forces of good and evil mentioned in Revelation 16. That the war was cast by contemporaries in apocalyptic terms is evident in Julia Ward Howe's "Battle Hymn of the Republic." The opening line strikes a millennial note, "Mine eyes have seen the glory of the coming of the Lord"; her subsequent descriptions of the conflict also invite apocalyptic construction. Abraham Lincoln, too, saw the conflict in ultimate terms. His second inaugural address expressed the hope that the "mighty scourge of war . . . speedily pass away," and yet if that did not occur, then "the judgments of the Lord" were "true and right," meaning the Almighty had some "purpose" in the terrible struggle.

But it was difficult for many in the aftermath of the Civil War to be confident that human efforts could carry forward the fortunes of the church. Many consumed with apocalyptic declared the reign of evil so pervasive and human efforts to alter the dire situation so ineffectual that the only hope for true believers lay in the dramatic intervention by Christ himself, who would return to Earth at the head of the armies of heaven and destroy the forces of evil. Then the saints would reign with Christ for a thousand years on Earth and subsequently follow the Day of Judgment. This version of the millennial hope, premised on explicit pessimism regarding human efforts to alter the situation, has been called premillennialism because Christ returns to the Earth before the beginning of the millennium.

One Protestant revivalist in the post–Civil War years who adopted premillennialism was Dwight L. Moody (1837–1899), a shoe salesman in Chicago who abandoned business for a religious vocation. His path went from Sunday school work to the YMCA, from there to a nondenominational church, and then to highly successful revivals both abroad and in the United States. Moody founded a Bible institute that nurtured others in his approach to scripture and to eschatology. He was explicit about his premillennial views: "I look upon this world as a wrecked vessel. God has given me a lifeboat and said to me, 'Moody, save all you can.'" Moody's apocalyptic views echoed through the ranks of conservative Protestants in the years that followed.

The expanding number and influence of conservative Protestants in the decades surrounding the turn of the twentieth century had implications for the spread of premillennial views. Debates over the interpretation of the Bible, the impact of modern science, and the place of the supernatural in Christianity divided Protestant communities in America. Conservative fundamentalists squared off against liberal modernists. Among the issues dividing them was also the embrace of premillennialism by the fundamentalists. That perspective often was combined with a dispensational view of history imported from Britain, where John Nelson Darby (1800–1882), one of the founders of the Plymouth Brethren, added to premillennialism the division of history into seven time periods or dispensations in which God's way of dealing with humankind changed. This dispensational view of history was structured into the influential Scofield Reference Bible first published in 1909. Premillennial dispensationalism posits Christ's return to the Earth to establish a millennial kingdom that is the seventh dispensation and the ultimate fulfillment of the apocalyptic hope. That view was widely adopted by conservative Protestants and melded into the fundamentalist perspective.

The disappointment that resulted from the failed predictions of Miller before the Civil War did not mean the end of hope for some of his followers. A number of the disappointed Millerites regrouped and from their ranks emerged new apocalyptically minded communities. One of the disappointed in 1844 was seventeen-year-old Ellen Harmon (1827–1915) who refused to surrender the notion of Christ's imminent return. She met and eventually married James White, an Adventist preacher. In concert with others of like mind, they developed a message regarding Christ's imminent return. But they did not single out a particular date. They also innovated in other ways, choosing to worship on the seventh day (Saturday). The Whites and others eventually formed the Seventh-day Adventist denomination. They achieved remarkable success, building educational, medical, and publishing institutions, at the same time never relinquishing their expectation of the imminent return of Christ.

The Adventist hope took a variety of institutional forms in late-nineteenth-century America. Another independent group founded by Charles Taze Russell (1852–1916), first called Zion's Watch Tower Bible and Tract Society, used the Bible to support radical Adventist positions. Decades later this movement was renamed the Jehovah's Witnesses. The Witnesses rejected a number of traditional Christian theological ideas, including judgments about Jesus and the sacraments as well as common social practices, including serving in the military and accepting blood transfusions. The primary responsibility of Witnesses is to "witness"—to proclaim their message, which includes a harsh indictment of many aspects of contemporary society. The message they disseminate is truly apocalyptic. From time to time Witnesses have also been willing to set dates for the end, a practice that repeatedly has had negative implications for the organization.

Pentecostalism, another new religious movement comprising a family of churches, emerged around the turn of the twentieth century. It was derived in considerable measure from the Holiness family of churches that had accepted dispensational premillennialism. In Pentecostalism gifts of the Spirit were featured, including the gift of prophecy. Pentecostals regarded the restoration of such gifts as a precondition of Christ's return at the start of the millennium. One Pentecostal denomination that featured the impending return of Christ was the International Church of the Foursquare Gospel founded by Aimee Semple McPherson (1890–1944). The "foursquare gospel" proclaimed a message of Christ as savior, healer, baptizer, and coming king. The last of these explicitly underscored Pentecostalism's millennial hope.

Other new religious movements arising in the early decades of the twentieth century also struck apocalyptic themes. The Peace Mission Movement founded by George Baker (ca. 1877–1965), an African American who took the name Father Divine, claimed that he was God come back to the Earth, fulfilling the prophecies of the book of Revelation, bringing peace, righteousness, and justice. The members of the Nation of Islam, founded by Wallace D. Fard (d. 1934?) and his successor Elijah Poole (1897–1975), renamed Elijah Muhammad, proclaimed a sharply contrasting apocalyptic message. The message to their followers, known as Black Muslims, was that the domination of blacks by whites was about to end with the impending destruction of white society and the ultimate vindication of blacks who were the original superior race. Elijah Muhammad declared Fard to be the incarnation of Allah.

The years since 1945 have witnessed little diminishment of interest in and commitment to the apocalyptic perspective in the United States. There has even been a general rise in the attention paid to apocalyptic as a result of diverse religious and cultural developments.

Premillennialism enjoys a broad base of acceptance among contemporary conservative Protestants, sometimes simply called evangelicals or fundamentalists. The Southern Baptist Convention, the largest Protestant denomination in the United States, and the variety of Pentecostal organizations are two communities where premillennialism prevails. The most respected evangelical voice in America, the evangelist Billy Graham (b. 1918), sounded apocalyptic themes in a 1983 publication entitled *Approaching Hoofbeats* that warned of nuclear, biological, and chemical threats that may precede the reign of Christ on the Earth.

Premillennial dispensationalism is also strikingly evident in contemporary America in other venues, including the megachurches that ring most municipalities and the cable-television programs that feature televangelists. Megachurches are independent congregations, many times embracing ten thousand or more members, presided over by powerful, charismatic preachers who combine conservative theology with a worship style that includes contemporary music. The theology from the pulpit often includes an explicit apocalyptic message. Some megachurches are also locations from which televangelists broadcast to viewers throughout the nation and the world. These powerful conservative preachers, including, for example, Jerry Falwell (1933–2007), Pat Robertson (b. 1930), and John Hagee (b. 1940), have exploited cable television with great success, thereby exercising astonishing religious, cultural, and political influence. Jack Van Impe (b. 1931) employs a different programmatic, but his weekly television broadcasts are even more explicitly apocalyptic as he and his wife, Rexella, examine contemporary news for evidence of the approaching end times.

Another medium fostering the apocalyptic mindset is the field of popular fiction. In 1970 Hal Lindsey (b. 1930) published the first edition of *The Late Great Planet Earth,* linking details in the book of Revelation with contemporary events throughout the world and especially the Middle East, a region at the time dominated by opposing powers, namely, the United States and the Soviet Union. The astonishing success of that volume set the stage for additional apocalyptic publications by Lindsey and others. The most remarkable example in this field is the series of *Left Behind* novels planned by evangelist Tim LaHaye (b. 1926) and authored by writer Jerry Jenkins (b. 1949). Beginning in 1995 with *Left Behind: A Novel of the Earth's Last Days* and including more than a dozen subsequent novels as well as all kinds of audio and children's spin-offs, the *Left Behind* series has made apocalyptic language commonplace throughout contemporary America, including the concepts of "rapture" and "tribulation," although many reading the more than seventy million copies sold may think of these stories as fiction rather than possible fact. Movies, too—apocalyptic and postapocalyptic films—are another popular medium through which apocalyptic views are disseminated.

In the closing decades of the twentieth century, a variety of new religious movements gained attention and notoriety in considerable measure because of their apocalyptic views. Often labeled by opponents as "cults," these groups frequently arose in relative obscurity and gained public attention only when some legal or criminal action occurred. Jim Jones (1931–1978), an ordained Disciples of Christ minister, led his expanding congregation, renamed the People's Temple, from Indiana to California, and subsequently to Guyana. Jones used his theology—a mix of Marxism, millennialism, and social activism—to fight segregation and racial injustice. In Guyana he hoped to establish a socialist community. Opponents in the United States as well as brutal repression and sexual violence in the community brought internal resistance to Jones and investigation from outside, resulting in Jones coercing and then leading more than nine hundred of his followers in a mass suicide/murder. Jonestown became a symbol for apocalyptic religion gone mad.

Adventism has spawned a number of splinter groups with distinctive apocalyptic themes. Mount Carmel, located outside Waco, Texas, was founded in the 1930s by Victor Houteff, a Bulgarian immigrant, after he was disfellowshipped by the Seventh-day Adventists. Houteff (d. 1955) was a prophetic figure who spoke of a future Davidic kingdom. After his death he was eventually succeeded by Vernon Howell (1959–1993), a convert who took the name David Koresh. Koresh set out to interpret the prophecies of the book of Revelation; he also fathered children by several young women. In 1993 an FBI raid intent on finding illegal firearms resulted in several deaths, both among the federal agents and members of the community. An extended, armed standoff complicated by hopeless misunderstanding about Koresh's apocalyptic mindset ended tragically, resulting in more than eighty deaths, including Koresh's. It appears that Koresh planned a peaceful resolution of the standoff after he finished interpreting the seven seals in the book of Revelation (Rev. 5–8).

The diversity among the groups featuring apocalyptic views is immense, as was evident in the case of the small community known as Heaven's Gate located in Rancho Santa Fe, California. In 1997 more than thirty members led by Marshall Herff Applewhite (1931–1997) committed group suicide, confident that they were departing into a higher realm where a spaceship would meet them. Applewhite identified with details in the book of Revelation. In the early 1990s he had predicted the end of the world. The members of Heaven's Gate viewed themselves as connected to prophecies contained in Christian apocalyptic texts.

Another community with distinctive apocalyptic ideas is the Unification Church founded in Korea by Sun Myung Moon (b. 1920). Moon, a visionary who believes he is to restore the kingdom of God on Earth, came to the United States in the 1970s. His followers regard him as a Second Messiah. He teaches that salvation will follow upon the creation of a God-centered family. Reverend Moon's own marriage is viewed as the foundation for that kingdom. Members of the Unification Church believe that the final struggle between good and evil is now underway and that ultimately Moon's task is to unite all religions. Moon and his community have aroused intense opposition at times.

Events in the recent past provide an instructive contrast with respect to apocalyptic visions and movements. In advance of the year 2000, speculation focused on possible dire implications of the turn of the millennium. In fact, however, Y2K predictions regarding bizarre religious behavior and catastrophic technological disasters proved unfounded. The new millennium began without apocalyptic implications. By contrast, the events of September 11, 2001, have reinforced the apocalyptic world view among a variety of religious groups in America and elsewhere. Many view the religious and military conflicts underway today in the Middle East, involving especially Israel and Iran, as evidence that we are living in a significant apocalyptic moment.

In this opening decade of the twenty-first century, a substantial number of Americans remain highly receptive to apocalyptic religious movements. The desire to know the future and the hope to be on the winning side of history contribute to this mindset. The astonishing diversity of apocalyptic views among those so committed apparently does not undermine their confidence. Therefore historians seeking to understand religious, cultural, social, and political movements should remain alert to the possible presence of such apocalyptic judgments.

The End of History; or, My Summer with Apocalyptic Christians

Nicholas Guyatt

There are real advantages to writing about dead people. They don't have blogs, so there's no danger that they'll see your work and grumble about what you've written. They can't send you personal messages correcting your mistakes or arguing with your tone. And you don't have that scratching sense when you write your book that the subjects may quietly read it and just feel bad about what you've said. As someone who has spent most of his short career writing about people who've been dead for a hundred years or more, I found out all of this when I decided to write a book about contemporary America. Before too long I felt quite nostalgic for archives and crumbling books and evidentiary dead ends. When you can find your subjects instantly via e-mail, no matter where you are in the world, you don't have the excuses upon which you normally depend.

In 2004 I had just finished my history Ph.D. at Princeton and got my first job at Simon Fraser University in Vancouver. My dissertation was on religious nationalism in early American history and especially on the cluster of ideas about providence and national purpose that suggested a divine mission for the United States. I'd placed my manuscript with Cambridge, and I was sure that I was writing a monograph rather than a trade book, but I had become fascinated by the disconnect between my work on American religious history and the currents of contemporary evangelicalism. To be sure there was still plenty of missionary rhetoric in American public life. George W. Bush used that language, and his speechwriter Michael Gerson had insisted on the role of providence in shaping America's momentous course through history. But this familiar language was at odds with a new conviction that was sweeping

From *Historically Speaking* 9 (May/June 2008)

through evangelical churches and bookstores. Tim LaHaye, coauthor of the bestselling *Left Behind* books, was telling anyone who would listen that God hadn't sent America to save the world, because the world wasn't going to be saved. It would be consumed by the Antichrist, and the end was approaching fast.

Would a historian have anything to say about the contemporary End Times movement? I was certainly curious about believers in biblical prophecy, and I felt an intellectual obligation to study them since they hadn't been big players in my providence manuscript. But I didn't want to muscle into the territory occupied by sociologists or religion scholars, who had already produced interesting monographs on *Left Behind* and on the upsurge of apocalyptic enthusiasm in America. My aims were a bit different. Could I take a few months off from my regular research and hit the road in search of the preachers and authors who were promoting the End Times message? Could I write a book that had some historical perspective but that threw light on the contemporary significance of apocalyptic Christians? More to the point: Would anyone be willing to publish it?

I found myself an agent in London, and he came up with simple suggestions about how to proceed. Write a proposal. Play up your historical knowledge, but don't become a prisoner to it. Look for a big thesis, and hammer it home when you map out your chapters. Boast that you're going to interview the colossi of the Religious Right, even if you have no idea how to contact them. I followed all these steps and let the agent do the rest. He quickly sold the book to Random House in the United Kingdom, and HarperCollins in the United States. Then, to my enormous surprise, he was fired from the agency. One of the things I've found out during my brief exposure to commercial publishing is that *every* author has a story to tell about his or her editor, publicist, mentor, marketing person, or jacket designer being fired at the *crucial* moment, just when the book was poised for enormous success.

Armed with a contract but no actual manuscript, I wondered how I'd meet my subjects. The hook in the proposal was straightforward: a Time/CNN poll recently found that nearly fifty million Americans believe that the events of the book of Revelation will take place during their own lifetimes. How does this affect their everyday lives? And should the rest of us be worried that they're looking forward to the end of the world? In the proposal I talked about the efforts of End Timers like John Hagee and Joel Rosenberg to influence Washington politics, particularly Middle East policy. But I also wanted to meet ordinary evangelicals who tried to live their lives in the shadow of the apocalypse. And I wanted to explain why this apocalyptic sensibility—

which was far removed from the main currents of American religious history—had come to prominence in recent decades.

Should I tell my prospective subjects that I was a nonbeliever and had serious doubts about the political lobbying of many apocalyptic Christians? I decided to call or e-mail a long list of pastors and evangelical authors. I told them the truth—or, at least, most of the truth. I was a historian who'd written an academic book about providentialism, and now I was writing a book for a general audience about apocalyptic Christianity. I was keen to explain the End Times perspective to nonevangelicals and to explore the history of prophecy in America. I was a lapsed Catholic rather than an End Times enthusiast, but I wanted to let my subjects speak for themselves.

By the summer of 2006 I had compiled an interview list that spread out across several states and a few weeks of travel. I still had gaps in my schedule, so I flew to San Antonio—the home base of Pastor Hagee—hoping to arrange more interviews on the fly. My first efforts were disappointing. I tried valiantly to get Pastor Hagee to speak with me, even crashing the reception for out-of-town visitors that follows the Sunday morning service at his megachurch. He smelled a rat, perhaps because I was European and a little too eager, and he sent me packing. But San Antonio was a great place to start because almost everyone else in town was happy to speak about Pastor Hagee. Each interview gave me a little more credibility, and people were willing to talk because I'd already spoken with their friends or colleagues. Before long the gaps on the calendar were filled, and I was meeting all kinds of apocalyptic Christians. I conducted about fifteen long interviews from Washington, D.C., to California. Within a month I had more than fifty hours of tape to transcribe and a much clearer idea of how the book would turn out.

I remember writing a paper in graduate school on Perry Miller, the celebrated historian of Puritanism, and planning a research trip to Massachusetts. When I spoke with my advisor about the sources for the paper, I focused on the Miller archives at Harvard but also mentioned a few of Miller's associates who might be happy to talk to me. My advisor shook his head and warned me against doing interviews. "They're sometimes helpful if you want to confirm something you already know," he said. "But don't rely on them to tell you things that you don't know." I realize that plenty of historians regularly ignore this advice and produce terrific books drawing on oral sources, but this warning stayed with me and informed my decision about how to write the book. I decided to arrange the chapters around the individual conversations I'd had and to steer clear of a big thesis or the kind of confident detachment that's expected from a monograph. Before making my research trip, I had a good grasp of the history of apocalyptic thinking in America and elsewhere. But I had no idea what was driving my subjects, and I retained this sense of uncertainty (and curiosity) as I wrote up my interviews.

One thing that I carried with me on my travels was the sense that my very limited sample of interviews made it impossible for me to speak with enormous authority about the apocalyptic movement. A more impressionistic approach to the writing seemed like a good idea not only because it might keep the reader entertained but also because a historian would be run out of town for making grand conclusions on the basis of a handful of conversations. I still feel a little uncomfortable, though, with the knowledge that some of my subjects agreed to talk because they believed that I was working within a different set of professional guidelines than most popular writers.

When I'd finished my interviewing and dashed off my first draft, events continued to defeat my expectations, which, after all, were based on my experience with academic—not commercial—publishing. My editors in London and New York were nice about my manuscript, but each thought that something was missing. One editor disliked my history chapters, in which I'd tried to offer a quick guide to the origins of prophecy belief and the role of apocalyptic thinking in America from the Pilgrims to World War II. "Can't you just drip-feed these into the other chapters?" he asked. He thought that the entire book should be a "journey": the reader should be on the road with the author from start to finish, and the story should move toward a big finale. This wasn't a whim or a quirk of this particular editor; when I looked through the publisher's Web site at the other books they'd recently done, I was shocked to see that they were *all* billed as "journeys." Even the cookery titles had a narrative arc, from the pantry to the fridge and beyond. I settled on a compromise, playing up the road-trip aspects while arranging my historical chapters as interludes between the traveling. But I was quickly made aware of one of the realities of commercial publishing: your book needs to fit within quite rigid guidelines of what sells and what doesn't. Historians who've published their historical work with trade presses are already familiar with this, of course. For the rest of us—who've learned to fear outside readers rather than editors—these nudges will be quite unfamiliar.

A more serious problem, according to both editors, concerned my tone and my perspective on evangelicals. Here was the advice, roughly speaking: "Could you make the Christians a little crazier?" I don't blame the editors for asking this question, because in my original proposal I had played up the potential threat of an organized evangelical lobby pushing its apocalyptic vision in Congress or even in the White House. I found some evidence for this frightening scenario on my travels, but I also realized that the contemporary apocalyptic movement is too diverse and complicated to be fitted into a simple Pastor Strangelove frame. This is perhaps the biggest dilemma I faced in working on the book: How much complication and nuance and uncertainty could I leave in the manuscript? Or, to put it differently, should a commercial publisher—drawn to a project by the overarching argument and the potential for a catchy headline—be in the business of subsidizing the more cautious thinking that our historical training encourages?

My editors had hoped for a snappy conclusion: "Fifty million Americans are trying to blow up the world, and President Bush is one of them!" I would have been happy to provide this, but my findings on the ground were rather different. Many influential evangelicals are indeed trying to hasten the apocalypse, and they've cleverly expanded their influence in Washington with a view to shaping America's Middle East policy. But most of those fifty million apocalyptic Christians are more ambivalent. Many have withdrawn from politics and worldly things. Some are trying to influence domestic policy (especially around the issues of abortion and education) but draw upon their End Times theology to structure their disappointment at political failure. Others can sustain completely separate visions of politics and theology, battling to influence local issues or to support national conservative candidates while acknowledging that some day the Rapture and the arrival of the Antichrist will make everything moot. Only a couple of my interviewees would venture details about the exact date of Christ's return; when they did, it was in hushed tones and with a variety of mathematical caveats.

I went into the project with a suspicion about the political influence of apocalyptic Christians in America and came out feeling fascinated by the intellectual and emotional burdens of Bible prophecy. Yes, some of these people are undeniably scary, and it's worth keeping tabs on the national leaders of the apocalyptic movement since they're more influential now than ever before. But I didn't find enough evidence to suggest that America was on the brink of a prophecy pandemic, so I didn't want to make that claim in the book. My editors were undoubtedly disappointed that I hadn't found a starker, scarier threat to liberal America, and I wonder if they would have commissioned the book on the basis of my eventual conclusions.

I am very grateful for the opportunity to write something rather different from my usual work. I've also been reminded of why some of the apparent disadvantages of history writing—the laboriousness of the research, the tendency to hedge your bets and to allow the evidence to emerge in all its complexity—offer a valuable alternative to the tight schedules and editorial imperatives of commercial publishing. Finally I've learned a valuable lesson from being able to meet the people I've been writing about. As I said earlier, it's unnerving to receive an e-mail from someone you've interviewed who has now read your book and isn't entirely happy. But visiting people and spending time with them confound some of the easy conclusions that you might draw from their writing alone. This seems especially true when you're dealing with people whose views about the world differ wildly from your own. I'm trying to remember this now that I'm back in the safety of the archives.

PART 5

Religious Experience and the Limits of History

Abundant History

Marian Apparitions as Alternative Modernity

Robert A. Orsi

In spring 2005 Historically Speaking *ran a forum on Constantin Fasolt's* Limits of History, *followed in the July/August 2008 issue by a series of reviews of* Manifestos for History.[1] *Although very different in detail, both of these explored the limits of critical historical method and its epistemological underpinnings. This part of the current volume returns to this important topic, this time from the perspective of religious history. Robert Orsi, a past president of the American Academy of Religion, is widely recognized as one of the leading scholars of American religious history. In this forum*[2] *Orsi uses Marian apparitions to explore how historians often tame religious experience into "safe" explanatory categories. In the process he highlights the tension between absence and presence in contemporary religious historiography. Two historians respond.*

David Hume stated, in section 12 of *The Natural History of Religion:*

> I believe, indeed, that there is no tenet in all paganism, which would give so fair a scope to ridicule as this of the real presence.

The historical and cultural study of Marian apparitions and pilgrimages immediately draws us into the deepest contradictions of experience and imagination in the modern world. This was made eloquently clear to me many years ago, in 1976, when I stopped by chance in the town of Knock, in County Mayo, Ireland, to fuel my car. I asked the gas station attendant how it was that Knock boasted such an enormous church with a plaza built

From *Historically Speaking* 9 (September/October 2008)

for vast crowds, as well as its own airport. Do you not know what happened here, he asked me? I did not. Are you Catholic, he asked? I am, I said. Not a very good one then, he said. He condescended to explain that in August 1879 the Virgin Mary along with several other holy figures appeared near the church wall in Knock to a number of villagers that grew as the evening wore on to around fifteen. "Here," the gas station attendant ended his story, "the transcendent broke into time."

Here, the transcendent broke into time. The conjuncture of transcendence and temporality, the particularity of *here* with the no-place or beyond-all-places of transcendence, exemplifies the unexpected conflations within Marian devotions of categories normally (meaning normal within the languages of the modern world) held distinct. People journey to Lourdes to bathe in water from the spring that bubbled up miraculously from the spot at Bernadette's feet where the Lady told the girl to dig during the ninth apparition. It is *this* water, coming unexpectedly from dry earth, that people want to drink and to pour on their wounds. But then what do we make of the fact that Catholic pilgrims around the world journey to human-made replicas of the Lourdes grotto far from the European site to drink and bathe in the (ordinary) waters flowing from plumbing hidden in (more or less) artfully arranged rocks? Pilgrims almost always know that the waters at these other Lourdes flow from local reservoirs, but still they insist that these waters have healing powers.

Conflations and erasures abound. In the places where Mary is encountered, where the transcendent not only breaks into time but also gets involved in the nitty-gritty of people's affairs, the boundary between private and public experience is blurred. Pilgrims speak their fears and their most deeply held needs and desires aloud in the presence of others to images of Mary. The carefully maintained distances among bodies are erased as volunteers and family members offer the most intimate support for pilgrims who cannot walk, feed, bathe themselves, or take care of their bodily needs, carrying them the final yards toward the healing water. A heightened sense of intimacy exists among people, even among strangers, a sharpened awareness of vulnerability, exposure, and dependence. The boundaries of single subjectivities dissolve in these potent environments of desire and need, conscious and unconscious. On another level while Marian shrines have served as pivots of nationalist sentiment, the same shrines become international centers, where nationalist sentiments are eclipsed, at least momentarily, in the shared experience and expression of common need before the Virgin. The shrines create alternative publics of men and women in need and distress. These sites, in other words, are characterized by their multiple instabilities.

There is always an excess of expression and experience at Marian shrines—too many candles, too many statues and images, too many rosaries, too much desire and need, and too many souvenir stores hawking too many things. At Lourdes in the weeks after the apparitions, the townspeople and visitors began setting candles at the site, as many as fifty-eight in the small space by Easter Sunday of that year. Plaster images of Mary also started to appear there, four of them by April 26, to the chagrin of local authorities, and over the weeks the statues were ever more elaborately decorated.[3] The density of shops overflowing with many things to buy, the throngs of people pressing close together, the seemingly endless repetition of rosaries—these may offend visitors unprepared for excess at Lourdes.

What words or categories of interpretation are there for phenomena such as these? How do we talk about what happened, first at Lourdes (and at other sites where the transcendent breaks into time and comes face-to-face with humans in the circumstances of their everyday lives), and then afterward, as the result of what happened at Lourdes, there and at all the other Lourdes? How do we account for the excess?

The reality created at Lourdes, the reality that then moves out from Lourdes along pilgrimage routes, moves out in the circulation of holy water and other souvenirs, and in the reproductions of the shrine itself, this reality is at fundamental odds with modern ways of knowing and interpreting the world. The boundaries that Mary's presence disrupts are the very ones modernity holds dearest. How is the event at Lourdes even approachable from outside the metaphysical assumptions underlying the phrase "the transcendent broke into time," a metaphysics the denial of which is fundamental to modern reason? The anomalousness of Marian apparitions and pilgrimages to modern historiography might have provoked a confrontation with the limits of modern knowing. Instead Marian apparitions and pilgrimages have been effectively and safely positioned in the last several decades within the framework of modern historiography. Earlier historians largely ignored such phenomena, so this new inclusion is a step forward; and we have learned a great deal about how shrines such as Lourdes contributed to local and national histories. But the categories and boundaries of modern historiography retain their authority.[4]

Historians tell us that Marian apparitions and pilgrimages served the Vatican in its campaigns against liberalizing states in Europe, contributing to the development of the modern centralized papacy. Modern popes have been avid supporters of Marian devotions, shrines, and apparitions. Marian devotions (paradoxically) also worked to deepen emergent modern national loyalties by establishing experiential bonds between the local and the national.

(Lourdes has functioned this way in particular, just as it has contributed to the primacy of the papacy in Catholic emotions.) Marian shrines complemented developments in the history of modern medicine by supplementing what little that physicians were able to do to heal people and by offering an alternative to the ever-greater authority of increasingly professionalized doctors, especially for women and for poor people. Pilgrimages contributed to and benefited from advances in national transportation lines. Marian healing sites countered the authority of science and offered spaces and occasions for dissent. After the Second Vatican Council, Marian apparitions and piety challenged the modernization of the church and authorized the resistance of Catholics who objected to the changes. This has all been well established now for various Marian apparitions around the world. There does not seem to be much more to add to these narratives theoretically, only more case studies to add to the list.

But this all remains resolutely within the interpretive field of modernity. Subaltern historian Dipesh Chakrabarty identifies what he considers to be the two key assumptions of modern historiography: "The first is that the human exists in a frame of a single and secular historical time that envelops other kinds of time. . . . The second assumption running through modern European political thought and the social sciences is that the human is ontologically singular, that gods and spirits are in the end 'social facts,' that the social somehow exists prior to them." Marian devotions and apparitions are likewise translated into social facts, fitted into modernity's ontological singular. The poles of interpretive possibility are functionalist, on the one hand, antimodernist, on the other—Marian devotions either contribute to the making of the modern world or obstruct it.[5]

The alternative to this narrowed historical vision, Chakrabarty suggests, is to allow other realities to break into theory.[6] Likewise, philosopher of history F. R. Ankersmit argues for the liberation "of the history of historical experience from the heavy and oppressive weight of (the historian's) language and to unearth experience from the thick sedimentary strata of language covering it."[7] How do we break into this space, not to destroy it but to enlarge it? The whole orbit of Marian devotionalism—apparitions, shrines, pilgrimages, the relationships that develop at and around shrines and on pilgrimages, the proliferation of the original site of presence to other sites of presence, the things taken away from these sites and the circulation of these things, and so on—is a good place within which to begin to imagine a new historiography.

Before the advent of modern epistemology and before the arrival of "religion" within the boundaries of Enlightenment reason, the woods, homes, and forests of Europe, its churches, statues, relics, holy oils and waters, and its shrines were filled with the presence of spirits, pre-Catholic and Catholic (or some hybrid). Catholic sacramental theology maintained that Jesus Christ was really present in the elements of the Mass. Max Weber famously referred to all this as "enchantment" before naming the modern "disenchanted." To take sacramental bread out into the streets in a great golden monstrance—as Catholic rioters did, for example, on the first morning of the Saint Bartholomew's Day massacre—was to bring Christ himself out into the streets. The saints and the Virgin Mary were present in representations of them, and their presence suffused their relics and the places where they had been, too, and things touched to their relics and to these places. Catholic Europe was a culture of presence. These beings that were present to humans could be encountered, engaged, bargained with, excoriated, and brought to witness events in the lives of people and communities, for better and for worse. "There was a time when the gods were not just a literary cliché," writes literary critic Roberto Calasso, "but an event, a sudden apparition."[8]

But Western modernity exists under the sign of absence. Time and space are emptied of presence. Absence is strictly enforced by language, by reigning aesthetics, and by a normative sensorium (to borrow one of theorist Walter Ong's key words) to which the gods are not available by touch, taste, sound, or sight. Drained of presence, religious experience is remade in conformity with modern liberal notions of what "religion" is: autonomous, a distinct domain apart from other areas of life, private, in conformity with the causal laws of nature, reasonable, interior—all the things that Marian apparitions and what follows from them are not. Historiography follows suit. Historians have inherited an ontology in which all events derive their meaning from the social and which is aligned with the modern privileging of absence. If this were not so, then we would find a place for the gods in our histories of the modern world. We would not reframe those occasions when humans and the gods come face-to-face with each other (as they did at Lourdes) in the registers of either function or resistance.

This is not to say that presence disappeared immediately in the modern world. Charles Taylor identifies an early modern sensibility of divine presence in the cosmos and in society, in which "God is present as the designer of the way we live." Isaac Newton imagined a universe not only set in motion by its creator but requiring the creator's ongoing watchful presence for its proper maintenance and for its energy. But what this correction from early modernity suggests is that we need a richer vocabulary for "presence." Taylor distinguishes "presence" in the Newtonian sense just described from what he calls "the old model of presence," noting that this persisted longer in Catholic societies. It is this old presence (and presences) I am talking about but in the modern, supposedly disenchanted, world.[9]

Presence (in the old sense of the word) does not disappear from the experience of modern humans. Obviously not, because Lourdes occurred in the modern world, as did many other such events. People outside Europe also continued to come face-to-face with their gods, in Asia and Africa, as European missionaries discovered. Protestant missionaries labeled these practices of presence popish; Catholic missionaries, unable to disassociate themselves completely from the logic of presence, identified other people's face-to-face encounters with their gods as demonic. Catholics also fretted about the obvious similarity between their own practices and pagan worship. One result of the period of European missionary expansion was hybrid Catholic/indigenous expressions and experiences of presence, for example, the world of African/Caribbean spirits, in which the Virgin Mary has been directly involved. One could say that the parallel history of modernity, from one perspective, is the history of the ongoing eruption of presence into the spaces of its denial, to the transformation both of religious practice and imagination and the social world.

I am not saying, in other words, that experiences of presence are atavistic. I am especially not locating them as premodern phenomena in a linear narrative of modernity. Presences have been marginalized and disciplined since the sixteenth century, in Europe and everywhere that Europeans touched, but the presence of the gods has persisted, abundantly so, and now they appear to be thriving again throughout the contemporary postmodern world.

The problem is that we have no idea what to make of the bonds between humans and the spirits really present to them within the limits of our critical theories. In modernist arrangements of knowledge, this is the domain of theology (itself a marginal discipline within modernist arrangements of knowledge). But in order for us to enlarge our critical theoretical vocabulary, the presence of the gods and humans to each other in the varied spaces of their interactions with all the practices and things such encounters generated has to become the domain of critical theory, too, and of history. We can talk of the spaces and times of shrines and pilgrimages, of the circulation of ritual objects, and so on, but we have probably talked enough about all this now. Further theorizing along these lines is simply deflecting attention from the challenge of understanding how people meet their gods and how their gods meet them, how humans and their gods make their ways together through the challenges and excitements of life, how the gods become dwellers in this same modern history, independently of their human counterparts, and what they get up to, and what all this means for the social, political, and psychological life of the contemporary world.

These experiences of radical presence or realness I call *abundant events.* The question I want to pursue is how it is possible to study abundant events without translating them immediately into the safe categories of modernist historiography and without yielding to the understandable frustration and despair that there is no way to think outside the modernist historical categories. The point here is to see how far the limits of our critical historical knowledge can be pushed but not to abandon them all together. My enterprise is not theological, in other words, but theoretical. What is required is an abundant historiography. So what is an abundant event, which we already know to be characterized by excess, by the conflation of categories, by too much intimacy, exposure, and vulnerability—by too much?

Before the apparition at Lourdes became the subject of local controversy, before politicians, clergy, and scientists had staked out their positions, and before historians came along to remind us that similar events had occurred in the region before, that there was a local folkloric tradition of little people to which the woman in white belongs; before the trains started running on improved nationalized railroad track; before the souvenir shops opened; and before the water was shipped out in little bottles all over the world, there was the event of the face-to-face meeting of Bernadette and the woman in white who came to be identified as the Immaculate Conception. Before everything else there was the event of the presence of the human and the divine to each other. All the other things happened and continue to happen because of what happened to Bernadette and then to gradually expanding circles of kin and neighbors, circles that finally came to include millions of Catholics around the world. All this happened, in other words, because of the abundant event of presence, and all this is evidence of the event's abundance.

What identifies an abundant event in history and culture? One way to begin thinking about this is to examine apparitions of the Virgin Mary as fundamentally part of Marian devotional culture generally, pilgrimage and shrine culture in particular. Apparitions capture attention because of their dramatic nature, but as almost all historians who study them point out, in the culture within which apparitions take place there is nothing out of the ordinary about them (although this does not mean that when they occur, they do not take people by surprise). They are anticipated, longed for, and even expected. Seeing this allows us to look at apparitions alongside more prosaic examples of Marian devotion, including the simplest prayers and rosaries, as well as pilgrimages and shrine practices. What these phenomena share—from the water in Lourdes to the cheapest trinket sold in a souvenir shop—is that they are instances of the relationship between human beings going about the course of their days and the powerful supernatural figure of the Blessed Mother who is present to them. This is what draws people to pilgrimage: relationships and the promise of relationships.

Relationships were at the core of the Lourdes event. The young girl who stood before the apparitional figure brought to that moment her own history of difficulties with significant women in her life, including her mother and the woman who had been a surrogate mother but who later turned cruel and abusive toward Bernadette. Complex and long-standing relational histories connected the first cohort of spectators at the grotto, those who had the powerful emotional experience (in their own accounting) of watching Bernadette in ecstasy. Bernadette, the seer, was also their daughter, niece, cousin, neighbor, and servant, and now she was in intimate communication with a figure with whom they, too, had been in intimate communication over the years, whom they knew from their own lives, and who bore the stories of their relationships to her as well. To say this is not to "psychoanalyze" the moment, in the old psychohistory sense. It is rather to begin to establish the appropriate relational density within which the event arose. These relationships ultimately gave way, as they always do in devotional Catholicism, to things: devotions focus the relationship on things (rosaries, prayer cards, and so on); the things take on their meaning from the relationship. But the key here is the density of relationships, real and imaginary. So one of the first things to say about an abundant event is that it serves as a focusing lens for the intricacies of relationships in a particular area at a particular time, meaning for all the hopes, desires, and fears circulating among a group of people as these were taking shape at a certain place and a certain time.

This relationship between Mary and her devout is like other intimacies, but it is not exhaustively analogous to them. The difference is ontological: in Mary's company the devout enter into a relationship with a supernatural figure of great power and compassion who bends to them and attends to their needs and fears but who also chastises them and warns them of dire consequences should they not attend to her wishes in return. This element of danger is hidden behind Mary's love, but it is always there. The risk of Marian devotions comes from Mary's power and from the realness of Mary's presence to her devout. What is really real about the Marian event—at Lourdes and at its replicas—is the presence of the supernatural in relationship with humans and the power of the needs, fears, desires, and imaginings, conscious and unconscious, that this exchange unlocks. Danger is also the result of the very action of the imagination that occurs in devotional culture. The Blessed Mother comes alive in her connection to her devout; their lives enliven her, but she is also a figure independent of them, as other to them as she is connected to them.

In the unlocked environment of the devotional relationship, much becomes possible that otherwise is not. Place and time become fluid; representations and souvenirs of the relationship of presence bear its immediacy and efficacy; things come alive; and the ordinary levels and domains of experience are dissolved into each other. There is more. People's imaginations become larger and more efficacious in their actions on the world and on other persons. To borrow a phrase from psychoanalyst Christopher Bollas, writing about moments of unusual psychic intensity in the course of a day, in the really real of the devotional relationship there develops "a separate sense that reaches through the barriers exercised by the limits of consciousness."[10] This accounts for the dreamlike quality of intense devotional moments and for the new combinations of reality, new experiences and perceptions that become possible in the devotional world. Anthropologist Paolo Apolito has written powerfully of this dimension of the Marian apparition site at Oliveto Citra. "It was as if," he says, "the obviousness of everyday perception underwent a drastic overhaul and the world appeared composed of new presences in old forms. . . . All was left suspended between ordinary perception and the possibility that all of a sudden something might emerge from the depths of the unspoken, breaking out of the accustomed surface of things, creating an opening that might suck the everyday order into metahistorical reality."[11] Here, the transcendent broke into time.

Relationships of presence, the being face-to-face with each other, that arise in the devotional context—either between persons on Earth or between heaven and Earth, among the living or among the living and the dead, among persons as they are or with persons as they desire to be or are desired to be—likewise come under the power of the unlocked imagination. People are more accessible to each other (for good and for ill) in devotional culture, the boundaries of their bodies, minds, and souls less secure. People may become more understanding of the needs and sufferings of others, more compassionate, but also more intrusive, experiencing the intimacy of devotionalism as the occasion for asserting their own demands on others, as anyone who has been "prayed for" knows.

The abundant event, moreover, is not exhausted at its source. Presence radiates out from the event along a network of routes, a kind of capillary of presence, filling water, relics, images, things, and memories. "Routes" are not to be understood here simply as pathways of commerce or as networks of church affiliation and connection. The routes are formed and shaped by the abundant event: they develop through successive transactions among people wanting to share their experience of presence, and in this way the routes themselves become media of abundance. The routes of the really real, the conduits of presence out beyond the place where the transcendent broke into time, include the many images of Lourdes in people's homes and the water the devout carry away from the site (or acquire by mail or from friends), the small plastic bottles shaped like the Immaculate Conception, capped by a blue crown, and the water people carry away from the replicas in various sorts of less representational containers. The routes include the pathways that pilgrims follow, too, pulling them toward Lourdes and its copies.

What all this suggests is that there are people everywhere in the modern world who live in ways beyond the conceptual range of modernist epistemology and historiography and at an angle askew to normative modernity (while they function quite well amid the ordinary challenges of life, let it be added). Modern theory has intermittently paid attention to such persons, for the most part to record their passing, enrolling them as further evidence of the inevitability of modernity's pervasive disenchantment. Western intellectuals have now and then searched for people of presence in other lands, but this has been anything but an innocent enterprise. It has been undertaken in justification of colonialism (for its work in elevating people from the superstition of presence) and sometimes to appropriate presence as an antimodern resource for moderns themselves. (This need not have been an insincere quest, nor did it fail to have some positive outcomes, among them the rise of the science of comparative religion.) But what distinguishes the being-in-the-world of these figures, namely, their experience of presence, is denied, disciplined, and occluded. Even when modern seekers set out to appropriate presence for spiritual and psychological ends of their own, presence is lost or distorted. Again I do not mean presence in the laws of nature here or in the workings of the polity; I mean face-to-face presence of humans and gods to each other and what happens in such contexts.

That there are such people who live in a reality not completely encompassed by modern critical knowledge is a realization that eventually comes to anyone who has spent any time in shrines or who has observed people in relationship to their gods. So anthropologist Gananath Obeyesekere, whose fieldwork was in Sri Lanka, speaks of cultures "where other forms of the reality principle operate," establishing "a pathway . . . whereby fantasy can come out into open consciousness" and where it is tolerated in the light of everyday reason. Stanley Jeyaraja Tambiah, also an anthropologist working in South Asia, argues for "two coexisting mentalities in mankind everywhere," one under the sign of "causation," the other what Tambiah calls "participation." "Participation can be represented as occurring," writes Tambiah, "when persons, groups, animals, places, and natural phenomena are in a relation of contiguity, and translate that relation into one of existential immediacy and contact and shared affinities."[12]

We need to take caution here, however: both Tambiah and Obeyesekere remain fixed on the binary established by modernity, although they give it other names. As a result they wind up endorsing modernity's normative boundaries. Obeyesekere juxtaposes a reality-fixated West to a mystic East; Tambiah divides understanding from imagination. Chakrabarty's model of a kind of historical helix in which modernity and what I am calling presence twine around each other is better. But as my discussion of the event at Lourdes is meant to show, the event of presence has nothing fundamentally to do with modernity. Abundant events are not the story of modernity's dissent or not only and always this. Presence requires a history of its own, and experiences and practices of presence suggest the lineaments of that history. Marian devotions show us that a vocabulary of practice, understanding, and experience is required that is neither identical to nor derived from modern historiography.

Among the issues that remain open in the development of the notion of an abundant historiography is whether or not such an approach to events in the past requires a particular kind of historical sensibility on the part of historians. Ankersmit thinks so. "Historical experience," he writes in a discussion of Huizinga, "is the historian's response to 'the call' of the past," and "there is in the case of historical experience a 'communication' between the historian and the past excluding all that is not part of this most private and intimate communication." It is striking in this regard that on the very first page of the preface to her history of Lourdes, Ruth Harris alludes briefly to her own physical distress, noting that "my work on Lourdes became part of a personal voyage, an act of sympathy with nineteenth-century pilgrims." Visiting Lourdes Harris describes how her sense of being an alien at the shrine is slowly eclipsed as she gets caught up in the work of helping other pilgrims who cannot help themselves. She tells of "being directed to help a mother care for her adult son who was incontinent, paralyzed, blind and deaf." In the end, Harris says, she was not "converted"—although why is this even an issue?—but "the experience" of being there "completely changed my approach to the topic."[13]

In a very preliminary way we may conclude from this that abundant events that are not exhausted at the source and are characterized by the face-to-face experience of presence may very well draw the historian, too, into an unexpectedly immediate and intimate encounter with the past. I read Harris's relief at not being converted as an expression of the anxiety this possibility provokes among us, understandably so, given our training. But it may be that this is what abundant historiography is: the effort to write abundantly about events that are not safely cordoned off in the past but whose routes extend into the present, into the writing of history itself.

Notes

1. Constantin Fasolt, *The Limits of History* (Chicago: University of Chicago Press, 2003). Keith Jenkins, Sue Morgan, and Alun Munslow, eds., *Manifestos for History* (New York: Routledge, 2007).

2. This forum was sponsored by a grant from the John Templeton Foundation.

3. Ruth Harris, *Lourdes: Body and Spirit in the Secular Age* (New York: Viking, 1999), 87.

4. Among the excellent historical accounts of Marian apparitions and pilgrimages that have appeared in recent years, I want to mention: David Blackbourn, *Marpingen: Apparitions of the Virgin Mary in Nineteenth-Century Germany* (New York: Knopf, 1994); William A. Christian Jr., *Apparitions in Late Medieval and Renaissance Spain* (Princeton, N.J.: Princeton University Press, 1981) and (with a somewhat different focus but related) *Visionaries: The Spanish Republic and the Reign of Christ* (Berkeley, Calif.: University of California Press, 1996); Sandra L. Zimdars-Swartz, *Encountering Mary: From La Salette to Medjugorje* (Princeton, N.J.: Princeton University Press, 1991); Michael P. Carroll, *The Cult of the Virgin Mary: Psychological Origins* (Princeton, N.J.: Princeton University Press, 1986) and *Madonnas that Maim: Popular Catholicism in Italy since the Fifteenth Century* (Baltimore, Md.: Johns Hopkins University, 1992).

5. Dipesh Chakrabarty, *Provincializing Europe: Postcolonial Thought and Historical Difference* (Chicago: University of Chicago Press, 2000), 16.

6. Chakrabarty, *Provincializing Europe,* 20.

7. F. R. Ankersmit, *Sublime Historical Experience* (Stanford, Calif.: Stanford University Press, 2005), 14.

8. Roberto Calasso, *Literature and the Gods,* trans. Tim Parks (London: Vintage International, 2001), 6. The detail about Christ in the streets of Paris comes from Mack P. Holt, *The French Wars of Religion, 1562–1629* (Cambridge, U.K.: Cambridge University Press, 1995).

9. Charles Taylor, *Varieties of Religion Today* (Cambridge, Mass.: Harvard University Press, 2002), 66–67. On Newton, see Dorinda Outram, *The Enlightenment* (Cambridge, U.K.: Cambridge University Press, 1995), 40, et passim.

10. Christopher Bollas, *Cracking Up: The Work of Unconscious Experience* (London: Routledge, 2002), 47.

11. Paolo Apolito, *The Apparitions at Oliveto Citra: Local Visions and Cosmic Drama,* trans. William A. Christian Jr. (University Park: Pennsylvania State University Press, 1998), 107–8.

12. Gananath Obeyesekere, *Medusa's Hair: An Essay on Personal Symbols and Religious Experience* (Chicago: University of Chicago Press, 1981), 167; Stanley Jeyaraja Tambiah, *Magic, Science, Religion, and the Scope of Rationality* (Cambridge, U.K.: Cambridge University Press, 1990), 107.

13. Ankersmit, *Sublime Historical Experience,* 125; Harris, *Lourdes,* xiii, xv.

How Abundant Is "Abundant History"?

Thomas Kselman

Not very long ago a historian of modern Europe who chose to study Marian apparitions would have been committing professional suicide. As Robert Orsi suggests in his essay, this is no longer the case, for over the past generation a number of scholars, including several at distinguished institutions, have written well-received books on apparitions at Lourdes, Marpingen, Ezkioga, and other places as well.[1] Orsi admires the work of Ruth Harris, David Blackbourn, and William Christian Jr., but he is also dissatisfied with it. Historians have, in his view, worked too much within "the interpretive field of modernity." Rather than open themselves to a presence that would disrupt their assumptions, historians translate apparitions into social facts, a narrowed vision that fails to capture the richness of the religious experiences of visionaries and devotees.

Orsi's criticism needs to be taken seriously, for he has a well-deserved reputation as one of the most important interpreters of modern religion. In his work on devotions to Mary and St. Jude, he has explored with great sensitivity those who pray privately and engage in public devotion to the saints.[2] Orsi's scholarship is characterized by the complex interweaving of personal religious experiences with sharp analyses of the historical and cultural contexts that shape without determining the prayers and rituals of the people he studies. In his most recent book and in this essay, Orsi moves beyond his work as a historian/ethnographer in order to challenge scholars to rethink the categories that define their approach to religion.[3] Marian apparitions, and presumably other religious experiences, should be reconceptualized as "abundant events," a category that will allow scholars to break out of the constraints that limit their ability to grasp the rich, powerful, and elusive relationships

From *Historically Speaking* 9 (September/October 2008)

that bring together the transcendent and the temporal, heaven and earth, saint and devotee.

While I accept Orsi's general view that scholars struggle to make sense of Marian apparitions and similar "abundant events," I am not as critical as he is of the results of their work and not persuaded that his new category offers any effective guidance. Orsi's criticism of the limiting assumptions that operate in historiography resembles the argument made by Brad Gregory in a recent article in *History and Theory,* part of a general forum on the conceptualization of religion in modern scholarship. According to Gregory, "the underlying beliefs of the modern social sciences and humanities are metaphysically naturalist and culturally relativist, and consequently contend that religion is *and can only be* a human construction."[4] I wonder if Orsi and Gregory may be reading too much into the work of their colleagues and perhaps not making enough distinctions between those who in fact adopt the kind of reductionist scheme they describe and others who approach religious experience without fully articulated theoretical or theological frameworks, but who nonetheless treat belief and practice with sympathy and respect.

Some recent studies of Marian devotions seem more liable to Orsi's criticism (and to Gregory's) than others. Michael P. Carroll, for example, employs a thoroughgoing Freudian perspective in his analysis of Marian devotions. For Carroll, "identifying strongly with the Virgin Mary allows women to experience vicariously the fulfillment of their desire for sexual contact with, and a baby from, their fathers."[5] It seems unfair to place Carroll in the same school as William Christian Jr. Trained as a cultural anthropologist, Christian describes with great sympathy apparitions in Spain in the early modern period and the twentieth century. Like Orsi he is concerned with what happens when people meet God and the saints.[6] Christian does relate visionaries and devotees to their social and political contexts, but drawing such lines does not make him a reductionist or someone who has, in Orsi's words, "inherited an ontology in which all events derive their meaning from the social and which is aligned with the modern privileging of absence." Ruth Harris, in her work on Lourdes, is particularly attentive to the importance of physical suffering and gender in shaping reactions to the apparitions and miracles of Lourdes, but in doing so she never denies the "presence" that Orsi refers to, leaving open to the reader final judgments about the possibility that the transcendent broke through at Lourdes.[7] In the work of Harris, Christian, and other scholars, I do not see the dogmatism that Orsi criticizes but an approach that is empirical and ecumenical, one that narrates sacred events, contextualizes them with the tools of political history and the categories of class and gender but does not try to explain them away.

Historians may not be as narrow in their view as Orsi suggests, but his description of apparitions as "abundant events" does suggest that there is considerable distance between their approaches to apparitions and his. In order to explain his concept of abundance, Orsi turns to the most famous of all apparitions, when Mary appeared to Bernadette at Lourdes in 1858. The encounter between Mary and Bernadette is the essential starting point for Orsi, who writes that "before everything else there was the event of the presence of the human and the divine to each other. All the other things happened and continue to happen because of what happened to Bernadette and then to gradually expanding circles of kin and neighbors. . . . All this happened, in other words, because of the abundant event of presence, and all this is evidence of the event's abundance." Orsi is here forcing scholars to confront the ineffability of the sacred as it burst through at Lourdes, an issue that challenges all scholars who study apparitions there and elsewhere. Most of the historians Orsi cites deal with such encounters, some more sensitively than others. But they then shift their focus to the contexts that Orsi regards as secondary, the "everything else" that he dismisses in the passage just cited, which he understands to include: controversy among politicians, clergy, and scientists; local folkloric tradition; trains; souvenir shops; and all the other events and paraphernalia that grew up around Lourdes. All of this may be interesting, but for Orsi what is "really real about the Marian event . . . is the presence of the supernatural in relationship with humans and the power of the needs, fears, desires, and imaginings . . . that this exchange unlocks."

What is the basis for this judgment about what is "really real" about Marian apparitions? At least in this essay it seems that Orsi wants to make a sharp distinction between religious experience as "abundant event" and the agents and contexts that shape and surround Marian devotions, which are somehow less real. For Orsi, insofar as context matters, it is in order to approach more closely the original encounter—the "abundant event"—and all the subsequent encounters between people involved with Mary and, through her, with each other. Orsi writes that "the abundant event . . . is not exhausted at its source. Presence radiates out from the event along a network of routes, a kind of capillary of presence, filling water, relics, images, things, and memories. 'Routes' are not to be understood here simply as pathways of commerce or as networks of church affiliation and connection." I accept Orsi's point that it is important always to keep in mind the spiritual meanings that are at the core of Marian devotions, but the passive construction embedded in this passage, in which "presence" radiates out, causes me some concern. As Orsi's own work demonstrates so well, "presence" expands not on its own and not only because of the spiritual concerns and needs of devotees. Marian devotions radiate out as well because of the work of clergy, merchants, and politicians whose motives are complex.

Historians who are concerned with understanding Marian apparitions as they relate to a particular time and place may be more inclined than Orsi to shift their attention to the historically specific contexts within which they occur. They may also be concerned with "function" and "resistance," with the ways Marian apparitions work at times to support and at times to subvert social, political, and ecclesiastical hierarchies. But it is not clear to me why a concern with such issues necessarily excludes a concern for "presence" and why these different approaches cannot cohabitate to their mutual benefit, sometimes in the same work. A disciplinary difference may be in play here: religious studies scholars emphasize the personal and relational encounter of "presence," while historians are more attentive to context. The best work on religion, as exemplified in Orsi's books on Mary and St. Jude, clearly do both, and rather than the deficiency of modern historiography on Mary, I would emphasize its ability to complement the study of scholars of religion.

Perhaps I might also put in a good word for scholarship on Marian apparitions and shrines that focus less on the originating "abundant" event and more on the environment that shaped the development of the cult. The work of Stafford Poole does not show up in Orsi's notes, perhaps because Poole's historical research on the cult of Our Lady of Guadalupe casts significant doubt on the historicity of the apparition. Poole might fairly be labeled a positivist in his approach to Marian apparitions, but his careful and critical reconstruction of the seventeenth-century texts and ecclesiastical activity at the basis of the cult and his review of the controversy over the canonization of the visionary Juan Diego (in which he was an active participant) are an important contribution to the history of Our Lady of Guadalupe.[8] In her recent book on the commercialization of the shrine at Lourdes, Suzanne K. Kaufman explores not only the marketing of the shrine in the second half of the nineteenth century but also the intense debates surrounding the intersection of the sacred and the profane that troubled and titillated clergy, devotees, and anticlericals.[9] I wonder if Orsi's concept of an "abundant historiography" is capacious enough to allow room for such works.

Orsi's essay includes a paradox that he identifies without fully resolving. On the one hand we have "Western modernity" in which "time and space are emptied of presence. Absence is strictly enforced by language, by reigning aesthetics, and by a normative sensorium . . . to which the gods are not available by touch, taste, sound, or sight." But just a few paragraphs later we learn that the enforcement is after all not so strict, for there is a "parallel history of modernity" that traces "the ongoing eruption of presence into the spaces of its denial." This "parallel history" can be traced at Lourdes and at other sites of Marian apparitions and through other "abundant events." Where then do we find the "absence" imposed by "modernity"? I presume it is in the academy, but even there the recent work on Marian apparitions and Orsi's own career suggest that the policing is less strict than in the past. If this is so, it is in part because the "abundant historiography" of Marian apparitions that Orsi calls for, perhaps not as fully articulated as he would hope or as influential as it should be, nonetheless already exists.

In thinking about Orsi's essay, I recalled a passage from Marc Bloch's classic work on healing miracles, *The Royal Touch,* which lays out two contrasting approaches to religious events and then seeks to reconcile them. Bloch's categories of "romantic" and "Voltairian" do not match up perfectly with Orsi's "modernity" and "abundance," for both would probably be subsets of a modernist historiography. But I cite the passage nonetheless because of its call for inclusion and its generous tone, traits that I believe are implicit but not fully developed in Orsi's concept of "abundant event."

> For all religious phenomena, there are two traditional explanations. One—call it Voltairian, if you like—prefers to see the fact under study as the conscious work of an individual thought very sure of what it is doing. The other, on the contrary, looks rather for the expression of social forces of an obscure and profound nature; this might be called the romantic approach. For has not one of the great services of Romanticism been its vigorous accentuation of the spontaneous in human affairs? These two kinds of interpretations are only apparently in contradiction. If an institution marked out for particular ends chosen by an individual will is to take hold upon an entire nation, it must also be borne along by the deeper currents of collective consciousness. The reverse is perhaps also true: for a rather vague belief to become crystallized in a regular rite, it is of some importance that clearly expressed personal wills should help it to take shape.[10]

Notes

1. In addition to the books cited by Orsi in note 2, see John T. McGreevy, "Bronx Miracle," *American Quarterly* 52 (2000): 405–43; James S. Donnelly Jr., "The Marian Shrine of Knock: The First Decade," *Eire-Ireland* 28 (1993): 54–99. Although it does not deal with Marian apparitions, William Christian Jr., *Moving Crucifixes in Modern Spain* (Princeton, N.J.: Princeton University Press, 1992), explores similar phenomena with great sensitivity.

2. Robert Orsi, *The Madonna of 115th Street: Faith and Community in Italian Harlem, 1880–1950,* 2nd ed. (New Haven, Conn.: Yale University Press, 2002), and *Thank You, St. Jude: Women's Devotion to the Patron Saint of Hopeless Causes* (New Haven, Conn.: Yale University Press, 1996).

3. Robert A. Orsi, *Between Heaven and Earth: The Religious Worlds People Make and the Scholars Who Study Them* (Princeton, N.J.: Princeton University Press, 2005).

4. Brad Gregory, "The Other Confessional History: On Secular Bias in the Study of Religion," *History and Theory* 45 (2006): 137. Michel de Certeau made a similar point in *The Writing of History,* which first appeared in French in 1975. According to de Certeau, for historians, "comprehending religious phenomena is tantamount to repeatedly asking something else of them than what they are meant to say; to questioning them about what they teach us concerning a social status through personal or collective forms of spiritual life; to taking as a *representation* of the society what, from *their* point of view, *founded* that society. . . . Between their time and ours, the signifier and the signified have castled. We postulate a coding which inverts that of the time we are studying." *Writing of History,* trans. Tom Conley (New York: Columbia University Press, 1988), 138.

5. Michael P. Carroll, *The Cult of the Virgin Mary: Psychological Origins* (Princeton, N.J.: Princeton University Press, 1986), 59.

6. William A. Christian Jr., *Visionaries: The Spanish Republic and the Reign of Christ* (Berkeley, Calif.: University of California Press, 1996), *Apparitions in Late Medieval and Renaissance Spain* (Princeton, N.J.: Princeton University Press, 1981), and *Moving Crucifixes.* Christian's earlier work on Spanish shrines is also exemplary: *Person and God in a Spanish Valley,* rev. ed. (Princeton, N.J.: Princeton University Press, 1989).

7. Ruth Harris, *Lourdes: Body and Spirit in the Secular Age* (New York: Viking, 1999).

8. Stafford Poole, *Our Lady of Guadalupe: The Origins and Sources of a Mexican National Symbol, 1531–1797* (Tucson, Ariz.: University of Arizona Press, 1995), and *The Guadalupan Controversies in Mexico* (Stanford, Calif.: Stanford University Press, 2006).

9. Suzanne K. Kaufman, *Consuming Visions: Mass Culture and the Lourdes Shrine* (Ithaca, N.Y.: Cornell University Press, 2005).

10. Marc Bloch, *The Royal Touch: Sacred Monarchy and Scrofula in England and France* (Montreal: McGill-Queen's University Press, 1973), 48.

Abundant History

Protestantism and Alternative Modernities

Jane Shaw

In his provocative and innovative essay, Robert Orsi challenges historians of religion to write histories and theories of (religious) "presence," which he describes as "the breaking through into time of the transcendent." This challenges modern historiographies, which, he argues, either write out religion in the modern period or reduce its contribution to social and political features of modernity. Orsi's appeal for a history of presence "that is neither identical to nor derived from modern historiography" is based in a particular context—Marian apparitions in modern Europe—and is therefore confined to Roman Catholicism. As a historian of modern Protestantism, my questions are these: Has Orsi selected a moment in modernity when there happened to be a revival of religious experience and appeals to the experience of "presence" were especially strong? Is Orsi's model distinctly Roman Catholic in its time frame? Or does it require, rather, the reframing of modernity in terms of a quest for religious experience that goes beyond denomination? To put it another way, would such a history transcend time but essentially be a Roman Catholic history precisely because it ignores the particularity of the Protestant experience that is and was so profoundly tied to the emergence of modernity from a medieval world view? Or can such a history of presence transcend denomination and at the same time speak to the particularity of presence in modernity? Orsi writes that "the parallel history of modernity, from one perspective, is the history of the ongoing eruption of presence into the spaces of its denial, to the transformation both of religious practice and imagination and the social world." My argument is that there is an alternative modernity—

From *Historically Speaking* 9 (September/October 2008)

perhaps alternative modernities. Ongoing research on the history of Protestantism, especially heterodox Protestant groups, is increasingly suggesting the ways in which religious experience (encounters with "presence") was a vital part of many people's everyday experiences in nineteenth- and twentieth-century Anglo-American culture. While Roman Catholics experienced a host of Marian apparitions in late-nineteenth-century Europe, Protestants found themselves turning to spiritualism, theosophy, higher thought, as well as Pentecostalism, Mormonism, and numerous utopian and millenarian groups. In the last decade or so a wealth of scholarship has identified this burst of heterodox and sometimes more orthodox religious activity, the quest for religious experience at the heart of so much of it, and the ways in which people defined themselves as religious subjects. Historians of Protestantism, then, are writing a new modernity—maybe multiple alternative modernities.[1]

No one identified this phenomenon better at the time than William James in his *Varieties of Religious Experience,* given as the Gifford Lectures in Edinburgh in 1902. James began from the premise that human beings have a religious propensity; the human capacity to apprehend the divine is therefore, says James, fundamental. The primary agent for James is the human being who apprehends the divine, whereas for Orsi it is the "ongoing eruption of presence" (the divine) into the spaces of its denial. But Orsi and James are reaching at the same thing: raw religion. For James, this original experience, rather than institutional religion, was always the "real thing," while *necessarily* being the foundation of institutional religion. "Personal religion," wrote James, "should still seem to be the primordial thing, even to those who continue to esteem it incomplete."[2] Orsi hints at the same line of argument in his article when he writes that "before everything else"—before the apparition at Lourdes became the subject of local controversy and everything snowballed from there so that it became an international pilgrimage site—"there was the event of the presence of the human and the divine to each other." W. R. Inge, who gave his influential Bampton Lectures in Oxford in 1899 on the subject of mysticism, three years before James gave his Gifford Lectures on religious experience, put it this way: "Mysticism has its origins in that which is the raw material of all religion . . . namely, that dim consciousness of the beyond, which is part of our nature as human beings." He defined mysticism as "the attempt to realise, in thought and feeling, the importance of the temporal in the eternal, and of the eternal in the temporal."[3] In other words it is the transcendent breaking into time. We might see Orsi, in this article at least, as a descendant of that group of late-nineteenth- and early-twentieth-century scholars (which included Evelyn Underhill and Rufus Jones as well as James and Inge—though they neither necessarily agreed with each other nor thought of themselves as a group), who wished to find and define that raw experience of religion in modernity.

Or is Orsi's proposal only applicable to Roman Catholicism? Is his model distinctly Roman Catholic with regard to its time frame, its category of abundance, and its emphasis on the density of relationships that emerge from incidents of religious presence? For, after all, the history of modernity is utterly bound up with the history of Protestantism. The foundation of Protestant churches marks the emergence of what historians now call the early modern period. And the early modern to modern story is usually told in terms of the rise of the individual: as Protestantism allowed individuals to have a personal relationship with God, so, too, did privatization follow—not just of religion itself but of numerous other cultural practices, such as reading, as witnessed by the rise of the novel. Is Orsi really referring to Protestantism when he writes: "Drained of presence, religious experience is remade in conformity with modern liberal notions of what 'religion' is: autonomous, a distinct domain apart from other areas of life, private, in conformity with the causal laws of nature, reasonable, interior"? When he writes that there are "people who live in a reality not completely encompassed by modern critical knowledge," is he suggesting that they have bypassed modernity, somehow avoided the traps of modernity, including the potentially sterile individualism of Protestantism? Does the rise of Protestantism mark a sort of "Fall," an end to the bountiful innocence and abundance of religious-experience-in-community that *was* medieval Roman Catholicism? Is his desire to break out of modernist historiographical structures therefore a desire to avoid what Protestantism "did" and return to a paradisiacal "pre-Fall" narrative of religious experience? Are the abundant events and the routes of relationships he talks of, in his scheme, only Roman Catholic? That's a genuine question to Orsi.

My answer to that question is no. Abundance is a hallmark of many distinctly modern, Protestant religious phenomena. Think of the Methodists and other evangelicals swooning in tent revivals and the way such swooning caught on: one down, all down. Recall the spiritualist mediums who produced voices of all tenors and timbres, brought into Victorian parlors the wildest of spirits who knocked tables over and scandalized, titillated, and comforted middle-class séance goers, and, in their extraordinary production of ectoplasm, made their very bodies midwives of "presence." Abundant events of this character went on to produce more abundance and networks of routes, as Orsi puts it, as séance goers themselves practiced automatic writing and sought spiritual healing. Likewise communities and relationships were at the heart of many modern Protestant movements. We should not be too swayed by William James's emphasis on the individual nature of religious experience, for which he has been rightly criticized. In the late nineteenth and early twentieth centuries, Shakers, Mormons, and lesser-known utopian groups such as the Oneida Perfectionists, the Floridian Koreshan Unity Community, and the Christian Israelites all relied on community as the mainstay of their religious experience and, far from making religion an autonomous and distinct domain, apart from everyday life, fused the two absolutely. In such communities relationships were key and often cemented by abundant events of "presence." Likewise, as in devotional Roman Catholicism, relationships gave way to things, whether the distinctive furniture of the Shakers, the Book of Mormon, or, as in the case of the House of David in Benton Harbor, Michigan, a popular tourist resort and amusement park run along the lines of the group's religious principles.

Does it matter, though, that I am mixing the orthodox and the heterodox here? Can we really liken the events at Lourdes to the revelations of Mother Ann Lee that produced the Shaker communities? Can Bernadette's visions of the Virgin Mary be looked at alongside the wild activities of a spiritualist séance? If we are to write a history of abundant events, then I think the answer must be yes. William James happily mixed orthodox with heterodox experience in his *Varieties,* and he was right to do so, for that moment when he was writing marked a desire for "presence." Such a desire, counterinstitutional as it was and so often is, took no account of predefined notions of orthodoxy.

The late-nineteenth- and early-twentieth-century writers who identified a new sense of "presence" have since been criticized for being ahistorical in their treatment of religion and appealing to a core experience that transcends time and place. This criticism is often levelled at anyone who tried or tries to write about religious experience outside the dominant paradigms of modernity, precisely because such writing necessarily questions one of the predominant intellectual assumptions of modernity: namely, that "the transcendent" does not exist, for nothing can be beyond time. But the criticism itself falls into the old paradigms of modernity and repeats a pattern that Orsi wishes, rightly, to avoid. In short Orsi is onto something vital here, and his article sets an important agenda for historians of religion. The first test of his model of abundant history is whether it can accommodate Protestantism as well as Roman Catholicism, heterodoxy as well as orthodoxy. The second test is whether it can avoid the charge of ahistoricism and simultaneously account for encounters with presence across time while speaking of their particular manifestations in modernity.

NOTES

1. See, for example, Joy Dixon, *Divine Feminine: Theosophy and Feminism in England* (Baltimore, Md.: Johns Hopkins University Press, 2001); Alex Owen, *The Darkened Room: Women, Power, and Spiritualism in Late Victorian England* (London: Virago, 1989); Molly McGarry, *Ghosts of Future Past: Spiritualism and the Cultural Politics of Nineteenth-Century America* (Berkeley, Calif.: University of California Press, 2008); Leigh Eric Schmidt, *Restless Souls: The Making of American Spirituality* (San Francisco: HarperCollins, 2005); and Catherine L. Albanese, *A Republic of Mind and Spirit: A Cultural History of American Metaphysical Religion* (New Haven, Conn.: Yale University Press, 2007).

2. William James, *The Varieties of Religious Experience: A Study in Human Nature* (1902; New York: Longmans, 1952), 31, 3; W. R. Inge, *Christian Mysticism* (London: Methuen, 1899), 3, 5.

3. Ibid., 3, 5.

Further Readings

Alternative Religious Movements

Albanese, Catherine L. *A Republic of Mind and Spirit: A Cultural History of American Metaphysical Religion.* New Haven, Conn.: Yale University Press, 2007.

Bednarowski, Mary. *New Religions and the Theological Imagination in America.* Bloomington: Indiana University Press, 1989.

Carroll, Brett E. *Spiritualism in Antebellum America.* Bloomington: Indiana University Press, 1997.

Foster, Lawrence. *Women, Family, and Utopia: Communal Experiments of the Shakers, the Oneida Community, and the Mormons.* Syracuse, N.Y.: Syracuse University Press, 1991.

Jenkins, Philip. *Mystics and Messiahs: Cults and New Religions in American History.* New York: Oxford University Press, 2000.

Pike, Sarah M. *New Age and Neopagan Religions in America.* New York: Columbia University Press, 2004.

Stein, Stephen J. *Communities of Dissent: A History of Alternative Religions in America.* New York: Oxford University Press, 2003.

Asian Religion

Cadge, Wendy. *Heartwood: The First Generation of Theravada Buddhism in America.* Chicago: University of Chicago Press, 2005.

Ecklund, Elaine Howard. *Korean American Evangelicals: New Models for Civic Life.* New York: Oxford University Press, 2006.

Joshi, Khyati Y. *New Roots in America's Sacred Ground: Religion, Race, and Ethnicity in Indian America.* New Brunswick, N.J.: Rutgers University Press, 2006.

Kurien, Prema A. *A Place at the Multicultural Table: The Development of an American Hinduism.* New Brunswick, N.J.: Rutgers University Press, 2007.

Mann, Gurinder Singh, Paul David Numrich, and Raymond B. Williams. *Buddhists, Hindus, and Sikhs in America.* New York: Oxford University Press, 2002.

Williams, Raymond Brady. *Christian Pluralism in the United States: The Indian Immigrant Experience.* New York: Cambridge University Press, 1996.

Catholicism

Dolan, Jay P. *The American Catholic Experience: A History from Colonial Times to the Present.* Notre Dame, Ind.: University of Notre Dame Press, 1992

Gamm, Gerald H. *Urban Exodus: Why the Jews Left Boston and the Catholics Stayed.* Cambridge, Mass.: Harvard University Press, 1999.

Koehlinger, Amy L. *The New Nuns: Racial Justice and Religious Reform in the 1960s.* Cambridge, Mass.: Harvard University Press, 2007.

Matovina, Timothy M. *Guadalupe and Her Faithful: Latino Catholics in San Antonio, from Colonial Origins to the Present.* Baltimore: Johns Hopkins University Press, 2005.

McGreevy, John T. *Catholicism and American Freedom: A History.* New York: Norton, 2003.

Nabhan-Warren, Kristy. *The Virgin of El Barrio: Marian Apparitions, Catholic Evangelizing, and Mexican American Activism.* New York: New York University Press, 2005.

Orsi, Robert A. *The Madonna of 115th Street: Faith and Community in Italian Harlem, 1880–1950.* New Haven, Conn.: Yale University Press, 1985.

O'Toole, James M. *The Faithful: A History of Catholics in America.* Cambridge, Mass.: Belknap Press of Harvard University Press, 2008.

Tweed, Thomas A. *Our Lady of the Exile: Diasporic Religion at a Cuban Catholic Shrine in Miami.* New York: Oxford University Press, 1997.

Historiography, Debates, and Theory

Boles, John B. *Autobiographical Reflections on Southern Religious History.* Athens: University of Georgia Press, 2001.

Capps, Walter H. *Religious Studies: The Making of a Discipline.* Minneapolis, Minn.: Augsburg Fortress, 1995.

Chakrabarty, Dipesh. *Provincializing Europe: Postcolonial Thought and Historical Difference.* Princeton, N.J.: Princeton University Press, 2000.

Morgan, David. *Visual Piety: A History and Theory of Popular Religious Images.* Berkeley: University of California Press, 1999.

Orsi, Robert A. *Between Heaven and Earth: The Religious Worlds People Make and the Scholars Who Study Them.* Princeton, N.J.: Princeton University Press, 2005.

Prothero, Stephen. *Religious Literacy: What Every American Needs to Know—and Doesn't.* New York: HarperCollins, 2007.

Tweed, Thomas A. *Crossing and Dwelling: A Theory of Religion.* Cambridge, Mass.: Harvard University Press, 2006.

Islam in America

Clegg, Claude Andrew. *An Original Man: The Life and Times of Elijah Muhammad.* New York: St. Martin's, 1997.

Gomez, Michael. *Black Crescent: The Experience and Legacy of African Muslims in the Americas.* Cambridge: Cambridge University Press, 2005.

Haddad, Yvonne Yazbeck, and John L. Esposito. *Muslims on the Americanization Path?* New York: Oxford University Press, 2000.

Marr, Timothy. *The Cultural Roots of American Islamicism.* Cambridge: Cambridge University Press, 2006.

Smith, Jane I. *Muslims, Christians, and the Challenge of Interfaith Dialogue.* New York: Oxford University Press, 2007.

Turner, Richard Brent. *Islam in the African American Experience.* Bloomington: Indiana University Press, 1997.

Judaism in America

Cohen, Naomi W. *Jews in Christian America: The Pursuit of Religious Equality.* New York: Oxford University Press, 1992.

Diner, Hasia. *In the Almost Promised Land: American Blacks and Jews, 1915–1935.* Baltimore: Johns Hopkins University Press, 1995.

Grose, Peter. *Israel in the Mind of America.* New York: Knopf, 1983.

Neusner, Jacob. *Stranger at Home.* Chicago: University of Chicago Press, 1981.

Sarna, Jonathan. *American Judaism: A History.* New Haven, Conn.: Yale University Press, 2004.

Wertheimer, Jack. *A People Divided: Judaism in Contemporary America.* New York: Basic Books, 1993.

———, ed. *The Uses of Tradition: Jewish Continuity in the Modern Era.* Cambridge, Mass.: Harvard University Press, 1992.

Whitfield, Stephen. *In Search of American Jewish Culture.* Hanover, N.H.: University Press of New England, 1999.

Mormonism

Brooke, John L. *The Refiner's Fire: The Making of Mormon Cosmology, 1644–1844.* Cambridge: Cambridge University Press, 1996.

Bushman, Richard Lyman. *Joseph Smith: Rough Stone Rolling.* New York: Vintage, 2005.

Davies, Douglas J. *An Introduction to Mormonism.* Cambridge: Cambridge University Press, 2003.

Flake, Kathleen. *The Politics of American Religious Identity: The Seating of Senator Reed Smoot, Mormon Apostle.* Chapel Hill: University of North Carolina Press, 2004.

Mauss, Armand L. *The Angel and the Beehive: The Mormon Struggle with Assimilation.* Urbana: University of Illinois Press, 1994.

Ostling, Richard, and Joan K. Ostling. *Mormon America: The Power and the Promise.* San Francisco: HarperOne, 1999.

Shipps, Jan. *Mormonism: The Story of a New Religious Tradition.* Urbana: University of Illinois Press, 1985.

Native American Spirituality

DeLoria, Vine. *God Is Red: A Native View of Religion.* Boulder, Colo.: Fulcrum, 1973.

Harrod, Howard. *Becoming and Remaining a People: Native American Religions on the Northern Plains.* Tucson: University of Arizona Press, 1995.

Jackson, Robert H., and Edward Castillo. *Indians, Franciscans, and Spanish Colonization: The Impact of the Mission System on California Indians.* Albuquerque: University of New Mexico Press, 1996.

Kidwell, Clara Sue. *Choctaws and Missionaries in Mississippi 1818–1918.* Norman: University of Oklahoma Press, 1995.

Martin, Joel. *The Land Looks After Us: A History of Native American Religion.* New York: Oxford University Press, 2001.

McNally, Michael. *Ojibwe Singers: Hymns, Grief, and a Native Culture in Motion.* New York: Oxford University Press, 2000.

Schwarz, Maureen Trudelle. *Navajo Lifeways: Contemporary Issues, Ancient Knowledge.* Norman: University of Oklahoma Press, 2001.

Wenger, Tisa. *We Have a Religion: The 1920s Pueblo Indian Dance Controversy and American Religious Freedom.* Chapel Hill: University of North Carolina Press, 2009.

Politics and Religion

Allitt, Patrick. *Catholic Intellectuals and Conservative Politics in America, 1950–1985.* Ithaca, N.Y.: Cornell University Press, 1993.

Creech, Joe. *Righteous Indignation: Religion and the Populist Revolution.* Urbana: University of Illinois Press, 2006.

Foster, Gaines M. *Moral Reconstruction: Christian Lobbyists and the Federal Legislation of Morality, 1865–1920.* Chapel Hill: University of North Carolina Press, 2002.

Harding, Susan Friend. *The Book of Jerry Falwell: Fundamentalist Language and Politics.* Princeton, N.J.: Princeton University Press, 2000.

Hatch, Nathan. *The Democratization of American Christianity.* New Haven, Conn.: Yale University Press, 1989.

Lambert, Frank. *Religion in American Politics: A Short History.* Princeton, N.J.: Princeton University Press, 2008.

Noll, Mark A., and Luke E. Harlow, eds. *Religion and American Politics: From the Colonial Period to the Present.* New York: Oxford University Press, 2007.

Ribuffo, Leo P. *The Old Christian Right: The Protestant Far Right from the Great Depression to the Cold War.* Philadelphia: Temple University Press, 1983.

Protestantism

Balmer, Randall. *Blessed Assurance: A History of Evangelicalism in America.* Boston: Beacon, 1999.

Boles, John B. *The Great Revival, 1787–1805: The Origins of the Southern Evangelical Mind.* Lexington: University Press of Kentucky, 1972.

Butler, Jon. *Awash in a Sea of Faith: The Christianization of the American People.* Cambridge, Mass.: Harvard University Press, 1992.

Marsden, George. *Fundamentalism and American Culture: The Shaping of Twentieth-Century American Evangelicalism, 1870–1925.* New York: Oxford University Press, 1980.

Noll, Mark A. *America's God: From Jonathan Edwards to Abraham Lincoln.* New York: Oxford University Press, 2002.

Porterfield, Amanda. *The Transformation of American Religion: The Story of a Late-Twentieth-Century Awakening.* New York: Oxford University Press, 2001.

Roberts, Jon H. *Darwin and the Divine in America: Protestant Intellectuals and Organic Evolution, 1859–1900.* Madison: University of Wisconsin Press, 1988.

Sobel, Mechal. *Trabelin' On: The Slave Journey to an Afro-Baptist Faith.* Princeton, N.J.: Princeton University Press, 1988.

Stephens, Randall J. *The Fire Spreads: Holiness and Pentecostalism in the American South.* Cambridge, Mass.: Harvard University Press, 2008.

Sutton, Matthew Avery. *Aimee Semple McPherson and the Resurrection of Christian America.* Cambridge, Mass.: Harvard University Press, 2007.

Turner, John G. *Bill Bright and Campus Crusade for Christ: The Renewal of Evangelicalism in Postwar America.* Chapel Hill: University of North Carolina Press, 2008.

Wacker, Grant. *Heaven Below: Early Pentecostals and American Culture.* Cambridge, Mass.: Harvard University Press, 2001.

Weber, Timothy. *Standing in the Shadow of the Second Coming: American Premillennialism, 1875–1982.* Chicago: University of Chicago Press, 1987.

Race and African American Religion

Blum, Edward J. *W. E. B. Du Bois, American Prophet.* Philadelphia: University of Pennsylvania Press, 2007.

Butler, Anthea D. *Women in the Church of God in Christ: Making a Sanctified World.* Chapel Hill: University of North Carolina Press, 2007.

Chappell, David. *A Stone of Hope: Prophetic Religion and the Death of Jim Crow.* Chapel Hill: University of North Carolina Press, 2004.

Frey, Sylvia, and Betty Wood. *Come Shouting to Zion: African American Protestantism in the American South and the British Caribbean to 1830.* Chapel Hill: University of North Carolina Press, 1998.

Genovese, Eugene D. *Roll, Jordan, Roll: The World the Slaves Made.* New York: Vintage, 1974.

Gomez, Michael. *Exchanging Their Country Marks: The Transformation of African Identities in the Colonial and Antebellum South.* Chapel Hill: University of North Carolina Press, 1998.

Harvey, Paul. *Freedom's Coming: Religious Culture and the Shaping of the South from the Civil War through the Civil Rights Era.* Chapel Hill: University of North Carolina Press, 2005.

Higginbotham, Evelyn Brooks. *Righteous Discontent: The Women's Movement in the Black Baptist Church.* Cambridge, Mass.: Harvard University Press, 1993.

Irons, Charles F. *The Origins of Proslavery Christianity: White and Black Evangelicals in Colonial and Antebellum Virginia.* Chapel Hill: University of North Carolina Press, 2008.

Raboteau, Albert. *Slave Religion: The "Invisible Institution" in the Antebellum South.* New York: Oxford University Press, 1978.

Contributors

KATHLEEN GARCES-FOLEY is an assistant professor of religious studies at Marymount University. She writes on contemporary religion in America, immigration, ethnicity and racialization, and changing funeral practices. She is the author of *Crossing the Ethnic Divide: The Multiethnic Church on a Mission* (2007) and editor of *Death and Religion in a Changing World* (2006). Garces-Foley is currently studying the parallel efforts of Roman Catholics, mainline Protestants, and evangelicals to integrate churches across the country.

NICHOLAS GUYATT is a lecturer in the department of history at the University of York in England. In addition to *Have a Nice Doomsday: Why Millions of Americans Are Looking Forward to the End of the World* (2007), he is the author of *Providence and the Invention of the United States, 1607–1876* (2007).

THOMAS S. KIDD is an associate professor of history at Baylor University and a resident scholar at Baylor's Institute for Studies of Religion. He is author of *The Protestant Interest: New England after Puritanism* (2004), *The Great Awakening: The Roots of Evangelical Christianity in Colonial America* (2007), and *American Christians and Islam: Evangelical Culture and Muslims from the Colonial Period to the Age of Global Terrorism* (2008). He is working on two new books: *A Christian Sparta: Evangelicals, Deists, and the Creation of the American Republic* and *Patrick Henry: A Biography.*

THOMAS KSELMAN is a professor of history at the University of Notre Dame. In 2005 he served as president of the American Catholic Historical Association. He has published *Miracles and Prophecies in Nineteenth-Century France* (1983) and *Death and the Afterlife in Modern France* (1993). He is currently working on a book on religious liberty in modern France with the support of a National Endowment for the Humanities fellowship.

BRUCE KUKLICK is Nichols Professor of American History at the University of Pennsylvania. His most recent book is *Black Philosopher, White Academy: The Career of William Fontaine* (2008).

GEORGE MARSDEN is the Francis A. McAnaney Professor of History Emeritus at the University of Notre Dame. He has written several important books, including *Fundamentalism and American Culture* (1980), *The Outrageous Idea of Christian Scholarship* (1997), and *The Soul of the American University: From Protestant Establishment to Established Nonbelief* (1994). His *Jonathan Edwards: A Life* (2003) was a finalist for the National Book Critics Circle Award and won numerous awards including the Bancroft Prize.

WILFRED M. MCCLAY holds the SunTrust Bank Chair of Excellence in Humanities at the University of Tennessee at Chattanooga, where he is also a professor of history. He is the author of *The Masterless: Self and Society in Modern America* (1994), winner of the 1995 Merle Curti Award of the Organization of American Historians for the best book in American intellectual history, and editor of *Figures in the Carpet: Finding the Human Person in the American Past* (2007).

JOHN T. MCGREEVY is I. A. O'Shaugnessy Dean of the College of Arts and Letters and a professor of history at the University of Notre Dame. He is the author of *Parish Boundaries: The Catholic Encounter with Race in the Twentieth-Century Urban North* (1996) and *Catholicism and American Freedom: A History* (2003). He is currently working on a study of the nineteenth-century Jesuits and what they tell us about religious controversy, the "Catholic revival," and the transatlantic dimensions of American religion.

ROBERT A. ORSI is a professor of religion and the first holder of the Grace Craddock Nagle Chair in Catholic Studies at Northwestern University. He is the author of a number of books, including the award-winning *Madonna of 115th Street: Faith and Community in Italian Harlem, 1880–1950* (1985) and *Thank You, Saint Jude: Women's Devotion to the Patron Saint of Hopeless Causes* (1996). His most recent book, *Between Heaven and Earth: The Religious Worlds People Make and the Scholars Who Study Them* (2005), received an award for excellence in the study of religion from the American Academy of Religion.

JAMES M. O'TOOLE is Clough Millennium Professor of History at Boston College. He is the author of *Passing for White: Race, Religion, and the Healy Family, 1820–1920* (2002) and *The Faithful: A History of Catholics in America* (2008).

STEPHEN PROTHERO is a professor of religion at Boston University. He has written five books. His newest is the *New York Times* bestseller *Religious Literacy: What Every American Needs to Know—and Doesn't* (2007), which won a 2007 Quill Book award. His first, *The White Buddhist: The Asian Odyssey of Henry Steel Olcott* (1996) won the Best First Book award of the American Academy of Religion in 1997. *American Jesus: How the Son of God Became a National Icon* (2003) was named one of the top religion books for 2003 by *Publishers Weekly.*

LEO P. RIBUFFO is Society of the Cincinnati George Washington Distinguished Professor of History at George Washington University. He is the author of *The Old Christian Right: The Protestant Far Right from the Great Depression to the Cold War* (1983) and *Right Center Left: Essays in American History* (1992).

JONATHAN D. SARNA is the Joseph H. and Belle R. Braun Professor of American Jewish History at Brandeis University and director of its Hornstein Jewish Professional

Leadership Program. He has written, edited, or coedited more than twenty books, including the acclaimed *American Judaism: A History* (2004), winner of the Jewish Book Council's Jewish Book of the Year award in 2004.

CHRISTOPHER SHANNON is an associate professor of history at Christendom College. He is the author of *Conspicuous Criticism: Tradition, the Individual, and Culture in Modern American Social Thought* (1996) and *A World Made Safe for Differences: Cold War Intellectuals and the Politics of Identity* (2001). Shannon is currently completing *Bowery to Broadway: The Ethnic City in Classic Hollywood Cinema.*

JANE SHAW is Dean of Divinity and fellow of New College, Oxford, and teaches in both the history and theology faculties at the University of Oxford. Her most recent publication is *Miracles in Enlightenment England* (2006), and she is currently completing the history of an early twentieth-century heterodox millenarian community based in Bedford, England.

STEPHEN J. STEIN is Chancellor's Professor, Emeritus, at Indiana University's department of religious studies. He is the author of several books and essays on American religious history, including *Communities of Dissent: A History of Alternative Religions in America* (2003).

RANDALL J. STEPHENS is editor of *Historically Speaking* and coeditor of the *Journal of Southern Religion.* He is the author of *The Fire Spreads: Holiness and Pentecostalism in the American South* (2008). Stephens is coauthoring with Karl Giberson a book on evangelical Christian authorities.

JOHN G. TURNER is an assistant professor of history at the University of South Alabama. He is the author of *Bill Bright and Campus Crusade for Christ: The Renewal of Evangelicalism in Postwar America* (2008). His current project is a biography of Brigham Young.

Index